This book is dedicated to Fathers Steve Roberts, Nick Pagano and Linh Nguyen; the three wise men who have presented me with numerous gifts. Thank you for never giving up on me.

Copyright 2015
Printed and distributed by CreateSpace

All Scripture cited from the New American Bible (NAB). The Old Testament, copyright 1970 by the Confraternity of Christian Doctrine; Revised New Testament, copyright 1986; Revised Psalms, copyright 1991. Used with permission.

References taken from the *Catechism of the Catholic Church* (CCC) English translation for the US, copyright 1994. Used with permission.

Quotations from authors still living (Aurelio Voltaire) used with permission.

Contact Information for Author: freekforchrist@gmail.com

# Gothlic:
# The Testimony of
# a Catholic Goth

### By Shane
### "Reverend Leviathan"
### Jensen

# Gothlic
## The Testimony of Catholic Goth

Introduction...pg 2

My Journey towards Goth...pg 4

Goth is......pg 8

Your Body is a Temple...pg 18

My Journey towards God...pg 24

The Bible plus Tradition...pg 31

Deuterocanonicals...pg 41

Communion of Saints...pg 49

Mary...pg 62

The Eucharist...pg 83

My Journey as a Gothlic...pg 91

# Introduction

"What's up with those freaks wearing black and those guys in their black robes?" This is a question that many people have asked about Goths, Catholic priests and monks. There are quite a few misconceptions that people have about the Goth scene and the Catholic Church, and it just so happens that I belong in both categories.

Ironically, certain Christians will use different passages and verses from the Bible to attack both the Gothic subculture and the Catholic Church, so my being a "Gothlic" (i.e. Catholic Goth) brings me twice the persecution. As a Goth I get accused of worshiping Satan, as a Catholic I get accused of worshiping Mary; as a Goth I get condemned for looking like the dead, as a Catholic I get condemned for praying for the dead. The list goes on and on.

I find it very interesting that the Goth community is open to people of different races, religions and creeds, but mainstream society is not open to Goths; they deem us "too weird" and unworthy of respect.

I am also amazed that although the Catholic Church "accepts [Protestants] with respect and affection as brothers," and admits that "all who have been justified by faith in Baptism are incorporated into Christ," (*CCC 818*) there are still Protestants who refuse to acknowledge that Catholics are Christians. Some even go to the extreme of declaring the pope to be the antichrist and the Church as the Whore of Babylon spoken of in *Revelation*.

The purpose of this book is to clear up the misconceptions that one might have about these groups. I'm only going to discuss the topics that I get confronted with the most so some questions may remain unanswered. There are also a few chapters that are autobiographical to show how important the Church and subculture are in my life. And now I ask you, the reader, to open your mind and heart as I attempt to explain what Goth *really* is and what Catholicism *really* teaches and why.

# Chapter 1: My Journey Towards Goth

Even as a child I always seemed to be interested in the strange and unusual, drawn to the paranormal and unexplainable. When I tell people that Pee-wee Herman was my role model and that I watched *Pee-wee's Playhouse* religiously they usually say that explains a lot.

Growing up I spent a lot of time with my cousins, and while they were interested in sports, fishing and camping, I was a Nintendo nerd. My father and uncles were all very athletic whereas I was more artistic, and Dad was always disappointed that I wasn't good at sports. I also enjoyed weird movies like *Beetlejuice*, *Killer Klowns from Outer Space* and *Creepshow*, and I would watch *Tales from the Crypt* with my dad.

Monsters and vampires always held a fascination for me. In fact, my mother got me to stop sucking my thumb by telling me if I didn't stop then I'd get vampire fangs. As soon as I learned how to read I was interested in books about Bigfoot, the Loch Ness Monster, UFOs and the Bermuda Triangle. Being into different things made it difficult to fit in.

My parents divorced when I was seven, Dad suffered a brain injury two years later and Mom remarried a man who was abusive to me, verbally and physically. He didn't understand me and would call me a fag, queer, and tell me constantly that I was good for nothing. I would cry myself to sleep many nights, wondering why I couldn't meet his expectations. They separated when I was in high school, well after I was already considered a reject by him and my peers.

All throughout my career as a student I was a reject that hung out with other rejects; never with the "in crowd" or popular kids. In elementary school I was the fat kid with cooties, and I was bullied all the way up to high school. In order to be liked by the popular kids I would've had to like the mainstream trends and listen to popular music, and I tried to do that but I wasn't happy; it wasn't who I was. I always liked different things, especially when it came to music.

Music has always been one of my strongest passions. I was a band geek for seven of my twelve years in school. Dad raised me on classic and alternative rock bands like Kiss, AC/DC, Pink Floyd and Alice Cooper. The first musical artist I became a big fan of was

"Weird Al" Yankovic; I found him to be original, funny and well, weird. In middle school I was introduced to Insane Clown Posse, a group unlike anything I'd ever heard before. I couldn't compare them to any other band and their shock value really caught my attention. I was a devout fan for many years, bought their merchandise and had a closet full of ICP t shirts. But time goes on and people grow and change.

It was my sophomore year of high school that I was introduced to the Goth community. I loved the attire (black always being my favorite color), and the Goths that I met were very interesting and kind people. Many of them were also victims of abuse, rejection and isolation due to being different and they were great sympathizers. I saw a lot of myself in the culture and especially the music. The first Goth band I listened to was The Awakening; the music was beautiful and the lyrics were moving. I discovered more groups and fell in love with the scene.

Here were musicians singing about being rejected and embracing it rather than trying to change to please others; singing about struggling with negative emotions, depression and the desire to be loved, and acknowledging that it's okay to express your sadness rather than putting on a fake "happy mask" all the time. Here were musicians that spoke to my soul and enabled me to accept myself as I am, and I learned that to be different is not a bad thing.

I found my place in the Gothic subculture, and the part that it plays in my life has varied in extremities throughout the years, but it is forever a part of who I am today. There are those who accept and understand that, and there are those who do not accept any part of it because they do not understand, mostly because they do not know anything about the Gothic music scene.

## Chapter 2:

## Goth is...

    I'll never forget my first day at Asbury University, a Christian institution. I was sitting in the cafe reading when a fellow student came up to me with a very concerned look on his face.

    "So, yeah, why are you here?" He said somewhat politely.
    "Excuse me?"
    "What is a Goth doing at a Christian school? It doesn't make sense for a Goth to be at a Christian school."
    Clearing my throat and holding my peace I responded, "Well, what do you think you know about the Gothic subculture?"
    "Isn't it a religion?"
    "What?! No, man, sit down and let's talk..."

After talking for over an hour he apologized up and down and thanked me for opening his mind. Other students weren't as open, seeing as many of them attempted to "convert" me numerous times and others thought the only reason I was there was to collect blueprints of the school and blow it up.

Some people have this bizarre idea that Goths are part of a dark cult with the trinity of death, depression and Satan at the center of it; nothing could be further from the truth.

During the third and sixth centuries if someone said they were Goth it would mean they were part of the Germanic tribe, the Goths. They practiced a form of Norse paganism and were known for their ruthless acts such as plundering, pillaging and also rape, most notably being the invasion of Rome in 410AD. In fact, due to their brutal nature the term "Gothic" became synonymous with "Barbaric."

Nowadays when someone says they're Goth it means nothing of the sort; it just means you're part of the Gothic subculture. Essentially, a Goth is someone who is a fan of Gothic music and aesthetics, which usually entails wearing a lot of black. But persons and styles vary greatly in the scene, almost as much as denominations vary in Christianity.

Along with the music and aesthetics Goths also have a love for pageantry, poetry (especially Edgar Alan Poe), art and movies. Classic horror and sci fi are usually a favorite; anything containing Bela Lugosi or Boris Karloff. B movies and independent films also get a lot of attention. I myself am a huge fan of Bruce Campbell. And you normally won't find a Goth who doesn't like Tim Burton.

## The Music

Goth is a subgenre of post-punk that formed during the late 1970s. It was defined as a separate movement from punk rock during the early 1980s as it started to diverge more and more. You might say that while the punk bands were *mad* about the evil and injustice in the world, the Goth bands were *sad* about the evil and injustice. And Goth, as opposed to punk, combines dark, often keyboard-heavy music with introspective and dark lyrics. English band Bauhaus is usually credited with being one of the first Goth bands, while 45 Grave and Christian Death are viewed as the first American Goth bands.

Since its beginning over thirty years ago Gothic music has broadened quite a bit and contains many subgenres that are still ultimately considered to be Goth in origin; this includes "old school" Goth, deathrock, darkwave, ethereal, industrial, new wave and Goth-a-billy.

Deathrock and "old school" Goth retain a lot of their punk roots so it's much more alternative. Darkwave, on the other hand, tends to have more of an electronic element and can sometimes sound like 80s pop music, only scarier. (Think of a darker David Bowie or heavier Culture Club.) Goth-a-billy is pretty much just rockabilly music about monsters, zombies and classic horror movies.

Defining other subgenres can be difficult at times, as bands can't really fit into one genre. Some groups will have heavy guitars with opera-like singing, and others are instrumental and very classical in tone. Midnight Syndicate is a good example of a dark orchestra, and could be seen as classically inspired Gothic music.

Lyrically speaking, the subject matter varies from artist to artist but each one usually contains a common element: the darker aspects of life; death, depression, romance and feelings of isolation. Most of the time the bands are not glorifying or encouraging the negative emotions as much as they are acknowledging them as a part of life. It's more of a sharing of grief than a longing for it.

I tell Christians that if they want to get an idea of the lyrical content of Goth music without actually listening to it that they should just read Psalm 88; it's very dark and grim in tone. I would classify it as the "Gothic psalm" of the Psalter:

*Psalm 88*

LORD, my God, I call out by day;
at night I cry aloud in your presence.
Let my prayer come before you;
incline your ear to my cry.
For my soul is filled with troubles;
my life draws near to Sheol.
I am reckoned with those who go down to the pit;
I am weak, without strength.
My couch is among the dead,

with the slain who lie in the grave.
You remember them no more;
they are cut off from your care.
You plunged me into the bottom of the pit;
into the darkness of the abyss.
Your wrath lies heavily upon me;
all your waves crash over me.
Because of you my friends shun me;
you make me loathsome to them;
caged in I cannot escape;
my eyes grow dim from trouble.
All day I call on you, LORD;
I stretch out my hands to you.
Do you work wonders for the dead?
Do the shades arise and praise you?
Is your love proclaimed in the grave,
your fidelity in the tomb?
Are your marvels declared in the darkness,
your righteous deeds in the land of oblivion?
But I cry out to you, LORD;
in the morning my prayer comes before you.
Why do you reject me, LORD?
Why hide your face from me?
I am mortally afflicted since youth;
lifeless, I suffer your terrible blows.
Your wrath has swept over me;
your terrors have reduced me to silence.
All the day they surge round like a flood;

> from every side they close in on me.
> Because of you companions shun me;
> my only friend is darkness.

Darkness and struggles is not the only thing Goth bands sing about; you do have love songs filled with hope now and then. Other common subjects that artists cover are folklore, fantasy, mythology and even spirituality. Yes, there are Goth bands that contain Christian members (e.g. Batzz in the Belfry, Dark Valentine, Dead Artist Syndrome, Godscare and Leper among others).

**The Attire**

It's quite possible you're Goth if you have trouble finding matching blacks.

Gothic fashion is just as - if not more - important as the music. The diversity in the music carries over into the fashion as well.

It's not uncommon for a Goth to hear "You know Halloween's over, right?" I've heard it numerous times throughout the year. There was another time when I was visiting an old friar in a nursing home, he looked me up and down and asked, "Are you in mourning?"

The common element that's found in all Gothic attire is black clothing. It's been said that Woolite Dark is a Goth's best friend. But just because someone is wearing all black that doesn't necessarily mean that person is Goth. I mean, let's face it, priests and some monks wear all black. For that matter, there's not some unwritten rule that says all Goths must wear nothing but black clothes twenty-four hours a day, seven days a week. There are those who choose to do so, but you also find those who favor dark colors like purple, maroon, crimson red and even white at times. Every Goth has his or her own preference.

As I said before, the styles in Gothic fashion are just as diverse as the music. Some people in the Goth scene keep it simple and just stick to black t shirts and pants, while others favor period garb and look like they've come from the Renaissance. And there's always leather, flight jackets, combat boots and trench coats.

Other Gothic aesthetics include but are not limited to corsets, fishnet stockings and hair extensions. The jewelry that's worn could be rings or earrings in the shape of bats, skulls or spiders; cross necklaces (rightside-up or upside down), dog collars and lots of chains.

Gothic fashion also tends to be gender-bending, so it's not uncommon to see a guy wearing eyeliner, black lipstick, whiteface or nail polish. However, this is in no way a reflection of his sexual orientation. Sometimes a Gothic man will have more makeup on than the woman he's with, which led to another popular saying: It's quite possible you're Goth if it takes *you* longer than your girlfriend to "get ready."

## The Philosophy

The Gothic subculture attracts many different people for different reasons. Some come into it just because they think it looks cool, and there are those with deeper passions and reasons.

For me, the underlying philosophy of Goth is that it's okay to be different. Mainstream culture wants to determine what's attractive and what's not, what's "in" and what's "out;" they tell you, "This is all the rage. If you want to be popular, do this, wear that and listen to this kind of music." To go against all of the suggestions of mainstream culture does not make one less-than-human or unworthy of respect; Goths understand and embrace this. The Goth scene welcomes those rejected by the mainstream.

Goths also tend to be victims of abuse - physical and verbal - from the "upstanding" members of the mainstream society. They are met with ridicule and rejection for being different. But rather than change to fit the norm, it's better to continue being who you are regardless if that means being an outcast.

## The Stereotypes

*"All Goths are Satanists."*

I am living proof that is statement is completely false. All Goths are *not* Satanists. In fact, the Satanists that I have met over the years don't even consider themselves Gothic.

Because Goths are fond of dark music, clothes, etc. and darkness is sometimes associated with evil, it's only natural that one would assume that Goths follow the Prince of Darkness, Satan himself. But this is not the case. A Goth's religious/spiritual beliefs are separate from the music and wardrobe. I have met many Goths over the years that are Christian, Agnostic, Atheist, Wiccan and Buddhist; all separated in spirituality but joined together in our love for the culture.

*"Goths hate 'normal' people."*

I think it's more appropriate to say that Goths hate the fact that "normal" people refuse to accept them.

Goths are generally very accepting of people of different races, religions, creeds and sexual orientations. If someone who is not Goth does not judge them, then the Goth will normally get along with that person. But if a Goth is met with aggression from a mundane, it is likely that the aggression will be reciprocated.

*"Goths are always depressed and obsessed with death."*

Sadly, there are some Goths who fit this stereotype but for the most part it's completely untrue. Rather, Goths don't suppress or hide the sadness that they feel. Mainstream and Christian culture seems to treat sadness as improper and we're expected to be happy all the time, but Goths accept it as a part of human nature and as something that must be expressed.

Aurelio Voltaire, Gothic artist and author, said it best in his book *What is Goth?*:

*"Most people think that Goths are volatile freaks obsessed with death and gore. Don't be fooled. They're basically just melancholy, more likely to commit suicide than homicide. And for that matter, they aren't really sad all of the time; this is primarily just an act that empowers them with an air of mystery. The truth is that very few Goths actually kill themselves - they'd much rather contemplate suicide and then just write a really bad poem about it."*

**Problems Only Christian Goths Have**

- Having "normal" Christians not understand and "regular" Goths not understand.

- Being called a Satanist though you wear a gigantic cross.

- Having your non-Christian friends turn your cross upside down.

- Visiting a Christian university and half the student body crosses themselves as you pass.

- Visiting a new church and the security guard follows you from your car to the church because you are "suspiciously dressed."

- Having parents move their little children a few rows further away when you seat yourself in church.

- When the pastor talks about heathens in his sermon and everyone turns to look at you.

# Chapter 3:

# Your Body is a Temple

Goths are an easy target for judgment and condemnation. Though Jesus says " Judge not, and you will not be judged; condemn not, and you will not be condemned" (*Lk 6:37*), Christians tend to judge and condemn things that are misunderstood or different. Goths are especially condemned for their looks and attire even though "man looks on the outward appearance, but the Lord looks on the heart." (*1 Sam 16:7*)

I had a shirt specially made that says "Jesus was Gothic;" it has turned many heads and sparked many interesting conversations. If a Christian asks me about it I get a chance to clear up their misconceptions about the Goth scene; if a Goth asks me about it I get a chance to share the Gospel.  When I'm asked how Jesus was Gothic I bring up these points:

•He was despised and rejected by men.

•He was a man of sorrows, familiar with suffering.  (*Is 53:3*)

•He was in the company of sinners and outcasts.  (*Mt 9:10-13*)

•The religious authorities accused him of being possessed by Satan.  (*Mt 12:24*)

•He was pierced.  (*Zech 12:10*)

Well, maybe that last one is a stretch since he wasn't pierced in the same way as some Goths are pierced, but it's easy to see how the life of Christ could inspire more Goths to embrace Christianity and relate to this Son of Man who is familiar with being rejected and misunderstood.  However, a lot of Goths want nothing to do with church because of being met with bitterness and hypocrisy by church goers.  It's hard to believe in a God of love and grace from people who only seem to preach hatred and judgment, and numerous verses are used to condemn.

*Lev 19:28:*  You shall not make any cuttings in your flesh on account of the dead or tattoo any marks upon you: I am the Lord.

What I find most entertaining about this verse being taken out of context is the fact that there are other verses in the same chapter that go completely overlooked.  The verse right before it forbids trimming your beard, and yet I've never seen a Christian condemn a man for being clean-shaven.  And just a few verses before that it says "Do not wear clothing woven out of two kinds of material" *(Lev 19:19)*, but I'm sure Christians wear polyblend and will not burn in hell for it.

The commandment forbidding tattoos was not given because the art of tattooing in and of itself is sinful, but rather it's the religious significance they had at the time.

Israel was to be a nation set apart and distinct from other nations, especially in their religious practices. Israel's pagan neighbors practiced self-mutilation as a part of their worship and mourning rites. Self-inflicted wounds (cutting, branding and tattooing) were symbolic of self-sacrifice and used as an extreme method of grabbing the attention of the deity. This can be seen in Elijah's challenging the prophets of Baal when they began cutting themselves (*1 Kgs 18:28*). Tattoos were also used in the occult and were thought to contain magical powers, and Israel was forbidden from practicing magic.

In this day and age, tattoos hardly have the same meaning as they did for ancient Israel; they're just a form of body art and nothing more.

*1 Cor 11:14:* Does not nature itself teach you that for a man to wear long hair is degrading to him?

If this is a universal law then we better destroy every painting, portrait and sculpture of Jesus since he's always depicted as having long hair. Oh, and don't forget the movies.

Paul's arguments are so directly based on the customs of that culture that his conclusions must be understood in that context. He also mentions that it's shameful for a woman to have short hair and that it's disrespectful to go without a veil (*1 Cor 11:6*), but a lot of Christian women have short hair and don't wear veils. Does that sound like a double standard?

In a Graeco-Roman setting, if a man had long hair it was seen as improper and feminine. The meaning is similar for the case of wearing a veil; it was seen as immodest if a woman's head was uncovered. The veil was also a sign of submitting to the authority of the husband, who was the head of the household. So if a man had long hair or wore a veil, and a woman had short hair or went without one, it was a reversal of gender roles and frowned upon.

Long hair is not defined as a disgrace for men throughout the entire Bible. In other places it's defined as exactly the opposite: a vow of separation and special devotion to God. This is especially true of the Nazirite vow described in chapter six of *Numbers*.

When someone became a Nazirite he vowed to abstain from wine, grape juice and any other product of the grapevine; he was forbidden to go near a dead body, and he was not permitted to cut his hair:

*Num 6:5:* All the days of his vow of separation no razor shall come upon his head; until the time is completed for which he separates himself to the Lord, he shall be holy; he shall let the locks of hair of his head grow long.

The unusually long hair of a Nazirite was a physical mark of his special devotion to the Lord. John the Baptist and Paul are thought to have been Nazirites, and then there's the most famous of all, Samson, the Nazirite from birth who lost all his strength when his wife cut his hair while he slept. (I must say, if I woke up with a shaved head I'd probably lose my strength too.)

*Deut 22:5:* A woman shall not wear anything that pertains to a man, nor shall a man put on a woman's garment; for whoever does these things is an abomination to the Lord your God.

This is the same verse that's been used to argue that women should only wear dresses and skirts because pants are for men, therefore, women shouldn't wear them. That argument has been thrown out the window by most churches.

As I said before, it's not unusual to see Gothic men wearing eyeliner or other forms of makeup, and some will occasionally wear feminine garb, but it's not a reflection of sexual orientation. This is not a commandment against fashion.

Sexual purity is a subject that stressed in the Old and New Testaments, especially in the Torah with all its purity laws. The command was most probably intended to prohibit certain sexual perversions as transvestism and homosexual practices, most explicitly under religious auspices, another common practice in Canaanite religion.

*1 Cor 6:19:* Do you not know that your body is a temple of the Holy Spirit, who is in you and whom you received from God?

Probably the most favorite verse used by Christians to condemn others for how they present themselves and how they treat their bodies. This verse is more popular than the prohibition of tattoos because not only is this in the New Testament and therefore superior to the "old Law," but since it proclaims the body as a temple of God it can be used to condemn not only tattoos but also piercings, certain styles of clothing and even your diet.

Again, a closer look at this passage will bring out the context. Paul is talking about immorality towards the body, sexual immorality to be more specific. The body of a Christian, which is holy, should not be joined to the body of a prostitute, which is unholy. He talks of adulterers, homosexuals and prostitutes and reminds his readers that their bodies are not their own, but God's own dwelling, "So glorify God in your body." (*1 Cor 6:20*)

Am I not glorifying God in my body by getting tattoos, piercings and wearing clothing that other people see as abnormal? If someone walks up to me today and quotes that passage to me I just respond with, "Of course I know my body is a temple. Why do you think I spend so much time decorating it?"

# Chapter 4:

# My Journey Towards God

Religion was not a big part of my life growing up. Mind you, my parents were not non-believers but they also wouldn't have been described as devout believers either. I knew about God and I heard the name Jesus every now and then, and we celebrated Christmas and Easter; but for me that meant Santa Claus and the Easter bunny, not the birth and resurrection of Jesus Christ.

I received my first Bible from my grandparents on Christmas of 1989; a King James Version, red letter edition. I was only 4 years old so it would be another three years before I picked it up and attempted to read it, which was no easy task. I couldn't understand the Old English translation and would constantly set it back down. I wouldn't pick up another Bible for ten years.

Even my earliest memories of church are not good. Occasionally when my grandmother was babysitting me I would accompany her to the Baptist church that she attended. I had two options when I went with her: stay in the sanctuary, remain silent and still while hearing boring music; or go into the Sunday school class with the other children, whom I recall were very rude to me and would not include me in the activities. So my first experiences with church did not give me a good impression of Christianity; boring silent services and people who would not accept me.

Come middle school I was pretty much an agnostic. I started learning about other ancient myths and religions such as the Greek and Egyptian gods and goddesses. I asked myself, "What makes the God of the Bible any different from Zeus or Ra? Why are these other myths and stories of creation false but the stories in the Bible are true?" I was searching for answers but didn't think I'd find them in Jesus Christ. Christianity was no more true or false than Hinduism, Wicca or paganism.

I received a new Bible for Christmas in 1999, a translation that a 14 year-old could understand; it had footnotes and commentary that really spoke to me. It was also at this time that I learned the Bible was a collection of books and not just one book, so rather than try to read it cover to cover I was advised to begin reading the New Testament. I found a lot of what I read very interesting but also very unbelievable. I got to the point where I was thinking, "Okay, this part might be true but I'm not too sure about that part." I decided the best way to explore my questions would be to confront a believer.

The self-proclaimed Christians that I went to school with were not much help at all. I would get damned to hell for not believing in the entire Bible and they would condemn me for doubting the existence of God. I also saw a lot of hypocrisy. These students who were going to church on Sunday were the same ones that bullied the rejects and did many things that the Bible deemed sinful. When I attempted to find a church home I never received any type of welcome and I was judged by my appearance; normally I would find myself seated alone on the last pew. After many failed attempts at finding answers to my questions I decided that church and Christianity would not be a part of my life. I couldn't believe in a God of love whose followers showered me with hatred. But all that changed two years later.

In the month of November 2001 I had a vision. I awoke in the middle of the night, the time was 3:30am (I looked at my alarm clock) and I saw an angel floating above my bed. I was a bit terrified and the question "Did I die?" ran through my head. All I remember is this luminous figure saying "King of kings," and then I went back to sleep.

When I awoke the next morning I was confused to say the least. I needed to try and clear my head so I put on my headphones and went for a walk. As I was walking I came upon a church called Christ Centered Church and it just happened to be Sunday. Was this coincidence? I felt something – or Someone – urging me to enter the church. The service had already started but I went ahead and walked through the doors into the lobby. The secretary came out and greeted me, and I asked if there was someone I could talk to. She had me take a seat and then a Sunday school teacher by the name of Wayne McKnight met me, smiled and shook my hand and said, "Come on in to my classroom." I was shocked that I was being received with so much love. They were not bothered by my alternative style of dress and did not judge me.

I decided to return for the full service the next week to see if I would be met with the same type of heartfelt welcome. Again, I was greeted and not judged, and the message that Pastor Tommy Howard gave was very moving. I felt the love of God for the first time in my life, accepted Christ and was baptized two weeks later. I was an active member of the church for four years, bringing in my other friends who were in alternative subcultures and showing them that not all Christians were hateful, and also playing in a Christian hard rock band for three years called When Light Fades. Sadly though, I lost a lot of other friends who thought I had been brainwashed. I left the church after some disagreements with a few parishioners and then one year later, after much study and prayer, I was received in full communion of the Catholic Church in October 2006.

**Why Catholic?**

As Goths tend to be drawn to the distant past, being Gothic played a major part in my coming into the Church. (If it weren't for being abused by religion you'd think that more Goths would be open to Catholicism. I mean, as Catholics we worship a guy who rose from the dead and we eat his flesh and drink his blood.) There are traditions and customs that go *way back* that are still used during Mass and prayer. There are people that complain about Catholics being too involved in ritual, but personally I was very much attracted to it; attracted to being part of a Church whose traditions can be traced back to the first century and beyond. I was amazed when I discovered how much of a role that Tradition played in the Church and most especially in orthodox beliefs and understanding Scripture.

The word *catholic* means "universal" and it was used to describe the Church as a whole and to emphasize the oneness of believers; also to distinguish the true Church from the heretical sects that proclaimed to be Christians but had broken off from the orthodox beliefs.

Evidence suggests that Ignatius of Antioch is the first person to use the term *Catholic Church* in his *Letter to the Smyrnaeans*, written around 107AD to the Christians in Smyrna. He says, "Wherever the bishop shall appear, there let the multitude [of the people] also be; even as, wherever Jesus Christ is, there is the Catholic Church." Cyril of Jerusalem (c. 315-386) and Augustine of Hippo (354-430) and other early writers also further developed the use of the term "catholic" in relation to the Church.

It has been said that the most dangerous thing a Protestant can do is study Church history and this is indeed true. My first step in coming into the Catholic Church was studying theology at Asbury University. One of the things theology majors had to do was attend forums that the theology department would organize, and one of these forums had a Catholic priest as a guest speaker to clear up a lot of the misconceptions that Protestants have about Catholicism (and believe me, there were a lot of them at Asbury, myself included). This priest did not fully convince me but he gave me a deeper respect for the Church.

I began dating a girl early in 2006 who was a Protestant-turned-Catholic. I thought I'd be able to point out all the flaws in Catholic beliefs but most of the things I thought Catholics believed were just common misconceptions. I attended my first Mass with her and a sense of euphoria came over me at the celebration of the Eucharist, and then I learned about the belief in *transubstantiation;* that the bread and wine truly become the Body and Blood of Christ. The more I studied Church history and teachings, the more I found that they were what the ancient Christians believed all along. To quote St. Augustine in his *Confessions:*

*"I was certain that they were uncertain and since I had held them as certainly uncertain I had accused thy Catholic Church with a blind contentiousness. I had not yet discovered that it taught the truth, but now I knew that it did not teach what I had so vehemently accused it of. In this respect, at least, I was confounded and converted." (Book 6, Chapter 4)*

Learning more about Catholic doctrines and dogmas and discovering the truth behind Catholicism played a major part in coming into full communion with the Church, but another important factor in my decision rested on the community.

It has been estimated that since the beginning of the Reformation there have sprung over 25,000 different denominations and sects within Christianity. As soon as someone has a different interpretation of Scripture or a "new revelation from God," the result could be a new church and different ideas about Christ; "true Christianity" gets rediscovered.

There is only *one* Catholic Church, and despite the many trials and tribulations throughout history this Church has remained standing for over 2,000 years. People like to point out the not-so-good points in Church history and things that happen today (the Crusades, Inquisition, sex scandals, etc.), but we must remember that the Church is made up of imperfect human beings, so the history is not going to be clean. Even with the Church's low points and moral downfalls, it still stands united and one which I think is very impressive and inspirational.

So the biggest things that brought me into the Catholic Church were unity and oneness. (Not to mention the Gothic cathedrals and gargoyles.)

# Chapter 5:

# The Bible Plus Tradition

Despite what some people may think, the Bible did not drop down from Heaven one day ready-made. Nor was it written by one man all at once. It consists of numerous books, written by different authors over the course of many centuries. And before all of this was put into writing and compiled, believers in Old Testament and New Testament times relied on Tradition.

The doctrine of *Sola Scriptura* or "Scripture alone" did not originate until the fourteenth century and it did not become widespread till the sixteenth; it was completely foreign to the early Church. The only Scripture that the first generation of Christians had was the Old Testament, seeing as the writing of the books of the New Testament didn't begin until twenty years after the birth of the Church.

It has been estimated that the Crucifixion took place circa 27-30AD. With those dates in mind let's look at a few points regarding some of the writings of the New Testament:

- *1* and *2 Thessalonians* are thought to be the first letters written, dated 50-52AD.
- *Mark* is thought to be the first Gospel written, dated 64-70AD.
- *John* is said to be the last Gospel written, dated 90-95AD.
- *Revelation* is believed to be the final book written, dated 95-100AD.

So the final book of the New Testament as we have it today was not completed until seventy years after the Death and Resurrection of Christ. Of course, scholars continue to debate over dates and compositions, some being more conservative and others more liberal. But one fact that cannot be disregarded is this:

The canon of the Bible was not officially settled until the Synod of Rome (382AD), and the Councils of Hippo (393AD) and Carthage (397AD, 419AD); the Church did not have a complete Bible until late into the fourth century! Before that time there was much disagreement over which books should be included in Scripture.

Tradition was essential in the Church, especially in compiling the writings of the New Testament. For example, there were other Gospels and writings that claimed Apostolic authority but did not end up in the canon because they did not agree with the

Deposit of Faith or were not seen as Apostolic in origin. These include the *Gospel of Thomas*, the *Gospel of James*, the *Didache* and the *Epistle of Barnabas* among others.

The unwritten Word (Tradition) gave birth to the written Word (Scripture); the Church produced the Bible, not vice versa.

"*Sacred Tradition and Sacred Scripture, then, are bound closely together and communicate one with the other. For both of them, flowing out from the same divine well-spring, come together in some fashion to form one thing and move towards the same goal.*" *Each of them makes present and fruitful in the Church the mystery of Christ, who promised to remain with his own "always, to the close of the age."*

"Sacred Scripture *is the speech of God as it is put down in writing under the breath of the Holy Spirit.*"

"And [Holy] Tradition *transmits in its entirety the Word of God which has been entrusted to the apostles by Christ the Lord and the Holy Spirit. It transmits it to the successors of the apostles so that, enlightened by the Spirit of truth, they may faithfully preserve, expound, and spread it abroad by their preaching.*"

*As a result the Church, to whom the transmission and interpretation of Revelation is entrusted, "does not derive her certainty about all revealed truths from the holy Scriptures alone. Both Scripture and Tradition must be accepted and honored with equal sentiments of devotion and reverence." (CCC 80-82)*

**Tradition Condemned?**

One of my most memorable conversations about following Scripture alongside Tradition was with a man from my former Protestant church. He came up to me and said, "I don't know why you follow traditions that aren't in the Bible. For me it's the Bible only."

"Oh, really," I replied, "who wrote the *Gospel of John*?"

"Well, the Apostle John, of course."

"Okay and where does it say that?"

"At the end of the Gospel. It says those were the words of the disciple whom Jesus loved."

"And where is John identified as the beloved disciple?"

"Well, it doesn't say explicitly. It's just according to tra…"

"Uh-huh. That's what I thought."

Tradition is the only thing that identified John as the Beloved Disciple and author of the Gospel bearing his name, and the same goes for *Matthew, Mark* and *Luke*. (All of the Gospels were written anonymously.)

Whether they realize it or not, most Protestants do believe in and follow traditions not explicitly stated in the Bible. For example, the Lord's Day is traditionally celebrated on Sunday (the true Sabbath is Saturday); traditionally we celebrate Christmas on December 25 (the actual date of the birth of Christ is unknown);

traditionally three wise men presented the Child Jesus with gifts (*Matthew* doesn't state exactly how many there were) and traditionally they were kings (others believe them to be royal astrologers).

With traditions like these that are commonly followed by most Christians why are Catholics condemned for following Scripture and Tradition? The answer lies in a few verses of the Bible:

*Matt 15:3:* He said to them in reply, "And why do you break the commandment of God for the sake of your tradition?

*Mark 7:8:* "You disregard God's commandment but cling to human tradition."

*Col 2:8:* See to it that no one captivates you with an empty, seductive philosophy according to human tradition, according to the elemental powers of the world and not according to Christ.

These passages are usually cited by Protestants to demonstrate that the Bible and Jesus himself condemn the practice of following Tradition. Taken out of context they do seem to suggest that, but let's take a closer look:

*Matt 15:4-6:* "For God said, 'Honor your father and your mother,' and 'Whoever curses father or mother shall die.' But you say, 'Whoever says to father or mother, "Any support you might have had from me is dedicated to God," need not honor his father.' You have nullified the word of God for the sake of your tradition."

*Mark 7:10-13:* "For Moses said, 'Honor your father and your mother,' and 'Whoever curses father or mother shall die.' Yet you say, 'If a person says to father or mother, "Any support you might have had from me is *qorban*"' (meaning, dedicated to God), you allow him to do nothing more for his father or mother. You nullify the word of God in favor of your tradition that you have handed on. And you do many such things."

It becomes clear that Jesus is not condemning Tradition as a whole but, rather, tradition that goes against God's word and makes Scripture null and void. Jesus is attacking human tradition that uses God as an excuse to get out of covenantal duties, but the divine Tradition of Scripture honors those duties, it does not destroy them. Sacred Tradition is always in line with Sacred Scripture. It's also important to note that the Church makes a distinction between Tradition and traditions:

*Tradition is to be distinguished from the various theological, disciplinary, liturgical, or devotional traditions, born in the local churches over time. These are the particular forms, adapted to different places and times, in which the great Tradition is expressed. In the light of Tradition, these traditions can be retained, modified or even abandoned under the guidance of the Church's magisterium. (CCC 83)*

Along with the verse from *Colossians*, Paul has many other things to say about Tradition.

*1 Cor 11:2:* I praise you because you remember me in everything and hold fast to the *traditions*, just as I handed them on to you. (Emphasis added)

The word Paul uses for "tradition" here is precisely the same word Christ used in *Matthew*.

*1 Cor 15:3-7:* The tradition I handed on to you in the first place, a tradition which I had received myself, was that Christ died for our sins, in accordance with the scriptures, and that he was buried; and that on the third day, he was raised to life, in accordance with the scriptures; and that he appeared to Cephas; and later to the Twelve; and next he appeared to more than five hundred of the brothers at the same time, most of whom are still with us, though some have fallen asleep; then he appeared to James, and then to all the apostles.

Here Paul records an appearance of Christ to five hundred brothers and also to James, a tradition not found in the Gospels.

*2 Thess 2:15:* So then, brothers, stand firm and hold to the traditions which you were taught by us, either by word of mouth or by letter.

Paul commands them to keep traditions, either given by word of mouth (oral Tradition) or letter (Scripture), and later says to shun those who do not act according to Tradition:

*2 Thess 3:6:* Now we command you, brothers, in the name of our Lord Jesus Christ, that you keep away from any brother who is living in idleness and not in accord with the tradition that you received from us.

Tradition is not only supported by the Bible but also by the testimony of early Christians:

Athanasius (360AD): "Let us note that the very tradition, teaching and faith of the Catholic Church from the beginning, which the Lord gave, was preached by the Apostles and preserved by the Fathers, and it was on this that the Church was founded." (*Four Letters to Serapion of Thmius 1, 28*)

Origen (c. 230AD): "The teaching of the Church has indeed been handed down through an order of succession from the Apostles, and remains in the Church even to the present time. That alone is to be believed as the truth which is in no way at variance with ecclesiastical and apostolic tradition." (*Fundamental Doctrines 1, preface, 2*)

Scripture and Tradition go hand-in-hand; you cannot have one without the other. Following Tradition apart from Scripture nullifies the Word of God, and following Scripture apart from Tradition can lead to erroneous beliefs. Peter tells us that there are passages in Scripture "which are hard to understand, that uneducated and unbalanced people distort to their own destruction" (*2 Pet 3:16)*, and this is indeed true seeing as heretical movements based their doctrines on Scripture interpreted apart from Tradition. A good example of this is the case of Arius, the fourth century priest who declared that the Son of God was a creature and was not co-eternal with the Father.

Arius and his followers quoted verses from the Bible to "prove" their claims that Jesus was not divine. There are roughly thirty-seven passages that can be used to defend this (*Deut 6:4, Prov 8:22, Mark 10:18, Col 1:15, John 8:42, 14:28, 5:19* and *20:17* to name a few), and passages that seemed to support the doctrine of the Trinity were interpreted differently. Even though Arius had based his arguments on the Bible and compared Scripture with Scripture, he still arrived at an heretical conclusion.

If you ask a Protestant whether or not Arius was correct in his belief that the Son was created, he will most likely respond in the negative. Orthodox Christians believe that the Father, Son and Holy Spirit are three Persons but one God, and Scripture is used to support this. So why was Arius wrong in his interpretation? Because it goes against the Tradition handed down to us by the Church Fathers.

Along with the passages previously cited, *Revelation* has also been used to condemn Tradition:

*Rev 22:18, 19:* I warn everyone who hears the words of the prophecy of this book: if anyone adds to them, God will add to that person the plagues described in this book; if anyone takes away from the words of the book of this prophecy, God will take away that person's share in the tree of life and in the holy city, which are described in this book.

*Sola Scriptura* Protestants will cite these verses to demonstrate that God wanted nothing added to his Word, which includes any kind of traditions. That is not a very strong argument, seeing as it was referring to the book of *Revelation* itself and not to the entire Bible since it was written almost 400 years prior to the Bible being compiled. Also, *Deuteronomy* contains a similar verse forbidding the adding to or taking away from the Law (4:2), one of the reasons the Sadducees did not accept the Prophets or the Writings but only the Law as authoritative.

If Protestants still persist in using *Revelation* as a prohibition of Tradition and of adding to or subtracting from the Bible, accusing Catholics of adding to the Word, then they are also guilty of going against this command, seeing as the Protestant reformers subtracted seven books from the Bible which brings us to our next point: the deuterocanonicals.

# Chapter 6:

# Deuterocanonicals

It's not far from the truth to think that Goths are interested in many "questionable" things, especially when it comes to our music, fashion and literature. As a Christian Goth I was *very* interested in the questionable books of the original canon. I wondered what sort of information and inspiration, or lack thereof, caused them to be removed during the Reformation.

One of the first things I did upon entering the Church was I got a Catholic Bible and read the seven books that the early Protestant reformers removed. Upon reading these books I felt that they made a grave mistake by removing them.

The Catholic use of the word "Apocrypha" should be distinguished from the incorrect Protestant use of the word. The books that the Church rejected by the Council of Hippo belong to the Apocrypha, whereas Protestants use the word to designate the seven books found in the Catholic Bible.

The deuterocanonical ("second canon") books are those books found only in the Catholic canon. The protocanonical ("first canon") books are the books of the Old Testament accepted by both Christians and Jews. Both the Eastern Orthodox and Catholic Church use the Catholic canon.

The Jews living in the few centuries before Christ were divided into two groups: those that lived in Palestine and spoke Hebrew, and the large number of Jews scattered throughout the Roman Empire that spoke Greek. The Diaspora Jews relied on Greek translations of Scripture called the Septuagint, which means "seventy," based on the legend that seventy Jewish scholars translated the Hebrew text into Greek in Alexandria.

So why are these books not included in the Palestinian canon?

Before the coming of Christ, the Jews in Palestine re-examined and eliminated some of the books from the existing canon. The Pharisees set up four criteria to determine which books would be included in the revised Jewish canon: 1) They had to be in harmony with the Torah; 2) They had to have been written before the time of Ezra; 3) They had to be written in Hebrew; 4) They had to be written in Palestine.

This eliminated *Tobit* and parts of *Daniel* and *Esther*, written in Aramaic and probably outside of Palestine; *Judith*, probably originally written in Aramaic; *1 Maccabees* and *Sirach*, written after the time of Ezra; *2 Maccabees* and *Wisdom*, written in Greek; and *Baruch*, written outside of Palestine. By the first century AD the revised canon was generally accepted by all Jews.

The Church recognized the Jewish canon of the Greek-Roman tradition, or Septuagint, as its Bible. The New Testament quotes from the Septuagint and it wasn't until the Reformation that this canon was seriously challenged. The Septuagint contained the deuterocanonicals.

Before a "table of contents" was placed at the front of our Bibles there was much dispute in the early centuries as to what was to be considered inspired Scripture. The books in question were the deuterocanonicals of the Old Testament and the New Testament books of *Hebrews*, *James*, *2 Peter*, *2 and 3 John*, and *Revelation*. The Church called together councils to settle this dispute; the councils at Hippo (393AD) and Carthage (397 and 419AD) listed all of these books as Sacred Scripture. Then 1,100 years after the Second Council of Carthage Luther returned to the Palestinian canon, today's Protestant Bible.

However, unlike Zwingli, Luther did not completely eliminate the deuterocanonicals; they were placed between the Old and New Testaments as an appendix. They stayed in many Protestant translations for 300 years because they were recognized as being useful for moral instruction. In fact, the Protestant kings of England imposed the death penalty on anyone who tried to remove the deuterocanonical appendix. It wasn't until 1827 that the books were completely discarded, under the British and Foreign Bible Society.

Though Luther emphasized his "Scripture alone" ideology, when Scripture didn't agree with his doctrine he wanted to delete it (*2 Maccabees* provides support for belief in the communion of saints and purgatory, which Luther rejected). He dismissed the deuterocanonical books and also wanted to eliminate *Hebrews*, *James*, *Jude*, and *Revelation*, going so far as calling *James* an "epistle of straw." At one point he wrote, "The epistle of James gives us much trouble. If they will not admit my interpretations, I will make rubble also of it. I almost feel like throwing Jimmy into the stove." (*Luther, vol. 4, p. 317*)

Luther wanted to remove *James* because of his emphasis on being justified by faith alone, and we all know that St. James tells us that faith without works is dead (*Jas 2:14-24*). Luther also added the word "alone" to his German translation of *Romans 3:28* so that it would read "man is justified by faith [alone] apart from the works of the Law."

Not many Christians realize that some of their favorite passages in the Gospels are deuterocanonical and that their inspiration was in doubt many times in early Church history. This includes *Mark 16:9-20* deemed the longer ending of *Mark*; the passage that speaks of an angel strengthening Jesus in his agony and his sweat being like drops of blood in *Luke 22:43-44*, and the story of the woman caught in adultery in *John 8:1-11*, found in different places in different manuscripts; after *7:36* or the end of the gospel, or after *Luke 21:38* or at the end of that gospel.

What Christian today would not accept the story of the adulterous woman or the other deuterocanonical New Testament accounts? If all Christians can agree on the deuterocanonical New Testament passages, why not accept the Old Testament deuterocanonicals?

Other Christians will object that the deuterocanonicals are not inspired because if they were then Jesus or the other apostles would have quoted from them. Whether a book was quoted or not did not determine its inspiration. *Esther, Nehemiah, Song of Songs, Ecclesiastes* and *Ruth* are not quoted in the New Testament and they're still considered Scripture; the *Book of Enoch* and *Assumption of Moses* are quoted, and yet they're not part of the Bible. And there are passages in some of the deuterocanonicals that seem to be alluded to in the New Testament and in Church Tradition.

Of the seven additional books in the Catholic canon I found myself especially moved and inspired by four particular works: the *Book of Tobit, Book of Wisdom,* and *1 and 2 Maccabees.*

*Tobit* was written by an unknown author probably early in the second century BC. It combines elements of Jewish morality, piety and folklore making it a book that stands between the historical and wisdom literature. Originally written in Aramaic, the original of the book was lost for centuries, making the Greek translation the primary source. Fragments of the book in Aramaic and Hebrew were found at Qumran in 1955 and are in substantial agreement with the Greek text.

The book tells the story of a devout Israelite named Tobit who is living among captives in Nineveh. He was a grave digger (very Gothic vocation) that would bury fellow Israelites who were deprived of burial and was virtuous in his love for the poor. He suffers for his virtue and is finally blinded. He then prays for death.

Another character, Sarah, is a woman who has not-so-good luck on her wedding night(s). She was married seven times, but on her wedding night before they could consummate, a demon named Asmodeus would kill her husband. She is then accused of killing them and is grieved of the abuse. Sarah too prays for death. Goths could very much connect with being deprived of love and also being wrongfully accused.

God hears their prayers and sends the angel Raphael whose identity remains hidden, to heal them both. Ultimately, Tobit gets cured of his blindness and his son, Tobias, marries Sarah; Raphael subdues the demon and then everyone lives happily ever after. And when Raphael finally reveals his identity he says he is "one of the seven angels who enter and serve before the Glory of the Lord" (*Tob 12:15*). *Revelation* also speaks of the seven angels around God (*Rev 8:2*).

I have always been a fan of the wisdom literature and the *Book of Wisdom*, also called the *Wisdom of Solomon*, became a favorite after reading it for the first time. It was written around 100BC. The author remains unnamed, but he's believed to be of the Jewish community in Alexandria, Egypt. He wrote in Greek and styled it in Hebrew verse. Old Testament writings are reflected throughout his work and it's a great example of post-exilic Judaism in the inter-testamental period. There is one passage that I will share that many Church Fathers believed to be a direct prophecy and seems to be reflected in *Matt 27:41-44*. I dare anyone to not see Christ in these verses:

*Wis 2:12-20*: "Let us beset the just one, because he is obnoxious to us; he sets himself against our doings, reproaches us for transgressions of the law and charges us with violation of our training. He professes to have knowledge of God and styles himself a child of the LORD. To us he is the censure of our thoughts; merely to see him is a hardship for us, because his life is not like other men's, and different are his ways. He judges us debased; he holds aloof from our paths as from things impure. He calls blest the destiny of the just and boasts that God is his Father. Let us see whether his words be true; let us find out what will happen to him. For if the just one be the son of God, he will defend him and deliver him from the hand of his foes. With revilement and torture let us put him to the test that we may have proof of his gentleness and try his patience. Let us condemn him to a shameful death; for according to his own words, God will take care of him."

The two *Books of Maccabees*, placed last in the Douai version of the Old Testament, and between *Esther* and *Job* in others, recount the story of the Maccabean Revolt; the Jewish families and leaders that fought against the attempted suppression of Judaism by the Seleucid kings that persecuted the Jews in Palestine in the second century BC. The books take their name from the first leader of this revolt, Judas Maccabeus, son of Mattathias. I was amazed these were not a part of the Hebrew Scriptures seeing that they tell the story behind the celebration of Hannukah.

*1 Maccabees* was written around 100BC, most likely in Hebrew, but the original has not come down to us. The Church has an early Greek translation that is full of Hebrew idioms. The unknown author, probably a Palestinian Jew, was writing mainly to record the salvation of Israel that God accomplished through the family of Mattathias, especially through his sons Judas, Jonathon and Simon, and his grandson, John Hyrcanus. It is similar in style to *Judges* and the books that recount the acts of Samuel and David.

*2 Maccabees*, rather than being a continuation of the first book, is more like a spiritualized account of the events discussed in *1 Maccabees*. The author states that his work is an abridgment of a five-volume work by Jason of Cyrene, which has not survived. It seems the author's purpose is to give a theological interpretation of the events surrounding the stories of Judas Maccabeus. He speaks about divine intervention, the resurrection of the dead on the last day, and also offers support for the Catholic doctrines that will now be discussed: The intercession of the saints in heaven, and the power of prayers offered for the dead (Purgatory).

# Chapter 7:

# Communion of the Saints

I used to think that those of us in the Goth community were the ones most interested in the undead, death and those who have gone before us; I was wrong. Upon entering the Church I believe that Catholics have Goths beaten on that subject. Catholics pray for and to the dead, remember the dead in Masses, and even have patron saints of grave diggers (Anthony the Abbot), coffin makers (Stephen the Martyr) and funeral directors (Joseph of Arimathea). How much more Goth can you get?

## Intercession of the Saints

*The three states of the Church: "When the Lord comes in glory, and all his angels with him, death will be no more and all things will be subject to him. But at the present time some of his disciples are pilgrims on earth. Others have died and are being purified, while still others are in glory, contemplating 'in full light, God himself triune and one, exactly as he is.'" – CCC 954*

The Church is the Body of Christ, and as baptized individual believers we make up that *one* Body, and death cannot separate us from the Body of Christ. Those of us on earth are the Church Militant; we pray for one another here on this earth still living and we also pray for the Church Suffering (those who may be in Purgatory). All Christians believe that we can ask each other for prayers, and Catholics believe that we can also ask the Church Triumphant (those in Heaven) to pray for us as well.

I heard a Christian once yell, "All Christians are saints it says so in the word of God," challenging the Catholic doctrine of asking for the saints' intercession in Heaven.

The word "saint" literally means "holy one," and indeed all of God's people are called to be "holy ones" or saints. In many of his letters St. Paul addresses the Christians in the Church as saints. (e.g. *2 Cor 1:1*) So the Protestant was justified in saying that all Christians are saints.

Nevertheless, there are certain passages in Scripture that speak of saints in a much narrower, more glorified sense than the ones present in the Church on earth. Matthew's gospel mentions the saints who rose from the dead after Christ died on the cross (*Mt 27:52*); St. Paul speaks of the saints who will accompany Christ from Heaven when he returns (*1 Thess 3:13*), and passages in *Revelation* refer to saints who are now in Heaven praying to God (*Rv 5:8, 8:3*). It is in this latter sense that the Catholic Church honors those who have gone before us.

So how does the Church faithfully determine that particular saints are in Heaven?

In the process of canonization (the formal recognition of sainthood) there are various kinds of evidence needed before the Church declares a particular person a "saint." First, there must be a reliable testimony to the person's exemplary holiness, evidence that the person's life has drawn others closer to God, and lastly, documented miracles occurring after the person's intercession has been invoked.

(Let me clarify that just because someone hasn't "officially" been declared a saint, it doesn't mean that particular person is not in Heaven. The Church acknowledges that there are more saints in Heaven than can be known, which is why we celebrate All Saints Day; the time of honoring declared and unknown saints.)

Catholics honor and venerate the saints by art, iconography and statues, which some Christians declare an abomination:

*Ex 20:4-5:* You shall not carve idols for yourselves in the shape of anything in the sky above or on the earth below or in the waters beneath the earth; you shall not bow down before them or worship them.

God did not classify all forms of statues as idols. In the Hebrew language an "idol" was a statue of a god or a representation of a god that was specifically meant to be worshiped (e.g. the golden calf). In other passages of Scripture God actually commands the Israelites to make statues: The Ark of the Covenant was to have two cherubim made of beaten gold (*Ex 25:18-19)*; Moses made a bronze serpent and put it on a pole to heal those bitten by the fiery serpents (*Num 21:8-9),* and it was only later destroyed by King Hezekiah when Israel began worshiping it as a god (*2 Kgs 18:4*).

When Catholics bow down before statues or paintings of saints we are not worshiping the statue, but rather venerating the saint that is depicted. Very similar to when a person might kiss the picture of a loved one. That person isn't worshiping or loving the picture, but rather they are displaying their love for the person *in the picture.*

Some argue that Christ is the one mediator:

*1 Tim 2:5:* For there is one God, and there is one mediator between God and men, the man Christ Jesus.

Truly, the Son of God is the sole mediator between us and the Father, but as believers we are also co-heirs with Christ and we are encouraged to pray for one another. When we ask others to pray for us - whether in heaven or on earth – we are not substituting that person for Christ. Rather we are asking that person for their intercession and their prayers are joined with our prayers; we become co-workers for one another in the Body of Christ and all of our prayers go to the Head of the Body, Christ himself. Subordinate mediation is only possible because of Jesus Christ.

Other people believe that asking those who have died to pray for us is a form of necromancy, which is clearly forbidden in Scripture (*Deut 18:10-12*).

Necromancy is a form of magic that involves communication with the dead – either by summoning their spirit or raising them bodily – for the purpose of divination, or to receive secret knowledge or information about the future. The former King Saul practiced necromancy in the story of the witch at Endor:

*1 Sam 28:7-19:* Then Saul said to his servants, "Seek out for me a woman who is a medium, so that I may go to her and inquire of her." And his servants said to him, "Behold, there is a medium at Endor." So Saul disguised himself and put on two other garments, and went, he and two men with him; and they came to the woman by night. And he said, "Divine for me by a spirit, and bring up for me whomever I shall name to you." The woman said to him, "Surely you know what Saul has done, how he has cut off the mediums and the wizards from the land. Why then are you laying a snare for my life to bring about my death?" But Saul swore to her by the LORD, "As the LORD lives, no punishment shall come upon you for this thing." Then the woman said, "Whom shall I bring up for you?" He said, "Bring up Samuel for me." When the woman saw Samuel, she cried out with a loud voice; and the woman said to Saul, "Why have you deceived me?  You are Saul!"  The king said to her, "Have no fear; what do you see?"  And the woman said to Saul, "I see a god coming up out of the earth."  He said to her, "What is his appearance?"  And she said, "An old man is coming up; and he is wrapped in a robe."  And Saul knew that it was Samuel, and he bowed with his face to the ground, and did obeisance.  Then Samuel said to Saul, "Why have you disturbed me by bringing me up?"  Saul answered, "I am in great distress; for the Philistines are warring against me, and God has turned away from me and answers me no more, either by prophets or by dreams; therefore I have summoned you to tell me what I should do."  And Samuel said, "Why then do you ask me, since the LORD has turned from you and become your enemy?  The LORD has done to you what he spoke by me; for the LORD has torn the kingdom out of your hand, and given it to your neighbor, David.  Because you did not obey the voice of the LORD, and did not carry out his fierce wrath against Amalek, therefore the LORD has done this thing to you this day.  Moreover the LORD will give Israel also with you into the hands of the Philistines; and tomorrow you and your sons shall be with me; the LORD will give the army of Israel also into the hand of the Philistines."

Saul consulted a medium, rather than God, for guidance and asked her to conjure up Samuel's spirit so he could receive secret knowledge and for this he is condemned.  In asking for the saints' intercession we are not trying to summon their spirits from the grave; it is simply asking them for prayer in the same way we ask those on earth to pray for us.  The saints may seem dead to some but they are alive in Christ, for "he is not God of the dead but of the living; for to him all are alive." (*Lk 20:38*)

And just how can we be sure that those in Heaven are praying for us?

*2 Macc 15:12-16:* What he saw was this: Onias, who had been high priest, a noble and good man, of modest bearing and gentle manner, one who spoke fittingly and had been trained from childhood in all that belongs to excellence, was praying with outstretched hands for the whole body of the Jews. Then likewise a man appeared, distinguished by his gray hair and dignity, and of marvelous majesty and authority. And Onias spoke, saying, "This is a man who loves the brethren and prays much for the people and the holy city, Jeremiah, the prophet of God." Jeremiah stretched out his right hand and gave to Judas a golden sword, and as he gave it he addressed him thus: "Take this holy sword, a gift from God, with which you will strike down your adversaries."

*Rev 5:8:* And when he had taken the scroll, the four living creatures and the twenty-four elders fell down before the Lamb, each holding a harp, and with golden bowls full of incense, which are the prayers of the saints.

*Rev 8:3-4:* And another angel came and stood at the altar with a golden censer; and he was given much incense to mingle with the prayers of all the saints upon the golden altar before the throne; and the smoke of the incense rose with the prayers of the saints from the hand of the angel before God.

Aside from the Scriptural evidence there have been different accounts of people, Catholic and Protestant, who have experienced death for a few minutes and said they were in Heaven. These people all talk about the ability of those in Heaven to see us and that they pray for those on earth, but how could the saints hear thousands of simultaneous prayers?

*1 Cor 15:42-43:* So it is with the resurrection of the dead. What is sown is perishable, is raised is imperishable. It is sown in dishonor, it is raised in glory. It is sown in weakness, it is raised in power.

Those who have gone before us see God as he is, and though their bodies have not been glorified their souls have been. The Holy Spirit makes it possible for them to hear us, for we know that Christ grants great powers to those who love him.

Many books written about Heaven maintain that those in Heaven cannot be aware of people and events on Earth because they would be made unhappy by all of the suffering and evil, and therefore Heaven wouldn't truly be Heaven.

I find this argument very unconvincing. God clearly sees everything that happens in this world and all of the suffering and evil he witnesses does not diminish the fact that Heaven is still Heaven. And when a person dies and is joined with Jesus Christ I would expect that person's soul to feel *more* rather than less compassion for those on Earth. The most important factor to remember is that the present Heaven is different from the new Heaven that begins with Christ's judgment, where there will be no more suffering. And while those currently in Heaven may feel compassion and sorrow for those of us on Earth, they are also aware of God's presence and they witness the good that he brings about every day, and they look forward to the second coming of Christ just as we.

**Purgatory**

A friend of mine once asked me if I could describe the idea of purgatory to them, and what I thought it would be like. All I could think of was the scene in the movie *Beetlejuice* when all the souls of those who had died are sitting in the waiting room, waiting for their number to be called.

Of course the image that came into my mind is completely inaccurate. It is also inaccurate to think of purgatory as a "temporary hell" or a "second chance" given to those who denied God while on earth. "Purgatory" is simply the name given by the Church to describe the final purification that some must go through before entering into Heaven.

*All who die in God's grace and friendship, but still imperfectly purified, are indeed assured of their eternal salvation; but after death they undergo purification, so as to achieve the holiness necessary to enter the joy of heaven. – CCC 1030*

According to *sola fide* theology there should be no need of a final purification because once baptized a person is perfectly purified. This is understood in the sense that Christ's blood does not actually cleanse us, but rather covers us. The Catholic understanding is that when a person is baptized and enters the

Church they are truly cleansed of original and personal sin, but in our fallen human nature we fall into temptation and struggle with personal sin throughout our life and must constantly ask God for forgiveness. Christ forgives our sins and restores our communion with the Father, but we must still be purified of our attachment to earthly things, either in this life or in the life to come.

God doesn't purify us instantly in this life against our free will and I don't expect it would happen at our death. As a Protestant I believed that purgatory was a possibility. On a personal level, I struggled with an addiction to pornography. I would fall into temptation constantly, then feeling conviction I would beg God for his mercy and I would try to break free of the addiction; it became a cycle of events. I had a hard time believing that if I died God would send me straight to Hell since I truly desired to rid myself of the addiction out of love for him, and at the same time I couldn't understand how against my free will he would just wave a magic wand and thus brain wash me of this personal sin I constantly struggled with (and occasionally still do) so I wouldn't desire the pornography anymore.

"Purgatory," like "Trinity" and "incarnation," is a word that does not appear in Scripture but does have scriptural support.

*1 Cor 3:15*: If any man's work is burned up, he will suffer loss, though he himself will be saved, but only as through fire.

St. Paul speaks of those who will be saved but will suffer from a cleansing purgatorial fire. God's presence or holiness is described as a consuming fire (*Heb 12:29*) and is often accompanied by this image (e.g. the burning bush, the fiery chariot that took Elijah to Heaven, tongues of fire, pillar of flames). Fire can destroy, but it can also refine. The purgatorial fire can be seen as a refining rather than destroying fire like that which is used to describe Hell.

*1 Pet 3:18-19*: For Christ also suffered for sins once, the righteous for the sake of the unrighteous, that he might lead you to God. Put to death in the flesh, he was brought to life in the spirit. In it he also went to preach to the spirits in prison,

*1 Pet 4:6*: For this is why the gospel was preached even to the dead that, though condemned in the flesh in human estimation, they might live in the spirit in the estimation of God.

Who were these spirits in prison? They were not souls damned to hell, because no amount of gospel preaching would bring them out of their hate for God and love of self. These were the souls of those who died in godliness before Heaven was opened after the resurrection.

These passages show that a third state, one of neither Heaven nor Hell, existed. On a side note, there are many places in the Old Testament as well where Sheol is mentioned (*Ps 139:8, Am 9:2* to name a couple). Often it is mistranslated as "the grave" when really it was the place of the dead similar to the Greek notion of Hades; a state in which a person's soul was neither glorified nor condemned. Some would argue that the third state ceased to exist after Christ preached to them, but the Catholic position of purgatory has support in the ancient practice of praying for the dead.

*2 Macc 12: 44-46*: For if he were not expecting the fallen to rise again, it would have been useless and foolish to pray for them in death. But if he did this with a view to the splendid reward that awaits those who had gone to rest in godliness, it was a holy and pious thought. Thus he made atonement for the dead that they might be freed from this sin.

Judas prayed for his men who died *in godliness*, that they might be cleansed of sin, and the author calls it "a holy and pious thought." This lends support to the belief that one may receive atonement after death. One of the reasons this book is no longer included in the Protestant canon is because it supported the belief in purgatory and praying for the dead.

*2 Tim 1:16-18*: May the Lord grant mercy to the family of Onesiphorus because he often gave me a new heart and was not ashamed of my chains. But when he came to Rome, he promptly searched for me and found me. May the Lord grant him to find mercy from the Lord on that day. And you know very well the services he rendered in Ephesus.

St. Paul's friend Onesiphorus is almost certainly dead, yet he asks God's mercy to be upon him. Not surprisingly, many of the ancient Christian tombs also ask the living to pray for those who were buried within.

If purgatory was not a reality, there is no sense in praying for the dead. Our prayers would be unnecessary for the souls in Heaven and useless for the souls in Hell.

The Church teaches purgatory as a dogma and reality, and let me clarify that it does *not* teach that every Christian who dies has to go through the cleansing of purgatory before entering Heaven. Only those who die in the state of grace with a skewed self-love will go to purgatory. We do not know the state of a person's soul when they die, so it is good to pray for them because one day you and I may be the ones who are being prayed for.

# Chapter 8:

# Mary

To this day I am still approached by Evangelists who attempt to "deliver" me from the Gothic subculture. At times when I try to assure them that I am a baptized believer and a member of the Catholic Church, they gasp. It's worse than they thought. I'm not a Satanist; I'm a Mary-worshiping papist.

Probably the one question that Catholics get asked the most is, "Why do Catholics worship Mary;" the biggest misconception of the faith. Nowadays if someone *accuses* me of worshiping her rather than genuinely asking me because they're misinformed I respond, "We don't worship Mary, we only worship statues of her," and then walk away.

Before I entered into full communion with the Church I wanted a lot of questions answered, particularly regarding Mary. As a Protestant I had nothing against Mary, nor did I give her much thought.

Based on what we know about Mary from the Bible, she is viewed as a woman of great faith; the culmination of other great women such as Deborah, Ruth, Esther and Judith. She's the only person in the Gospels who witnessed both Christ's birth and crucifixion, and was with the disciples on the day of Pentecost.

Mary is acknowledged and honored as the first among believers, the Mother of the Church and our spiritual Mother since when the Son of God took on flesh he became our brother. The Church teaches that she was conceived without the stain of original sin (Immaculate Conception), remained a virgin throughout her life (Perpetual Virginity), was assumed bodily into Heaven at the end of her life and was crowned Queen of Heaven by her Son (Assumption and Coronation). It is beliefs like these that cause many Protestants to cringe.

**The Hail Mary**

*Hail, Mary, full of grace! The Lord is with thee; blessed art thou among women and blessed is the fruit of thy womb, Jesus. Holy Mary, Mother of God, pray for us sinners now and at the hour of our death. Amen.*

This is the most common prayer used by the Church to ask the Virgin Mother for her prayers. What may come as a surprise to some Protestants is that the first part of the prayer is taken from

Scripture: Gabriel greets Mary with the words, "Hail, full of grace, the Lord is with you!" (*Lk 1:28*); Elizabeth says to her, "Blessed are you among women and blessed is the fruit of your womb." (*Lk 1:42*) The part that bothers some people is calling Mary the Mother of God, even though Elizabeth refers to her as "the mother of my Lord." (*Lk 1:43*)

Some Christians object to calling Mary the Mother of God because they feel it implies that Mary is somehow above God or greater than him, when in fact exactly the opposite is true. The Church gave her this title in order to help people understand who Jesus Christ truly is.

In the earliest times of Christianity – continuing into the present – there was much confusion and disagreement concerning the Incarnation; those who denied the humanity of Christ and those who denied his Divinity. There were many variations ranging from the belief that Jesus was not God but a lesser, heavenly being (i.e. an archangel); or that the Divine Person joined himself to Jesus at his baptism and left right before his death.

The Church declared that from the moment of his conception to the end of his life, Jesus Christ was one Person with two natures, fully human and fully Divine. In becoming man Jesus took on a human body, mind and soul, but did not cease being God; his human nature is subordinate to the Divine nature.

"God sent his Son, born of a woman," (*Gal 4:4*) and that woman is who he received his humanity from. Mary is the mother of the one Person, Jesus Christ, who is the Son of God in the flesh.

Those who denied that she was the Mother of God were the same ones that denied the Divinity of Christ.

When I was in high school marching band we took a trip to New York City and one of the sites we visited was the famous St. Patrick's Cathedral. I found the church to be very beautiful and I got a Rosary as a souvenir; no intention of ever using it or even knowing how it's properly used. That changed two years later.

The Rosary has been a very powerful tool in my prayer life. I first felt that it was mindless repetition, but then I learned how to make it a true form of meditation and prayer, concentrating on the different mysteries that are the center of the Rosary. I found myself particularly drawn to the Sorrowful Mysteries (go figure). Being able to meditate upon the different times in my Lord's life (the agony in the garden, scourging, crowning of thorns, carrying the cross and crucifixion) made me experience them with him. Asking Our Lady to pray for me while focusing on those aspects of Christ made it clear to me that he suffers for and with me. And I also learned new Marian prayers that had some Gothic overtones ("mourning and weeping in this valley of tears").

**Immaculate Conception**

*"The infusion of Mary's soul was effected without original sin...From the first moment she began to live she was free from all sin."* – Martin Luther, sermon: *"On the Day of the Conception of the Mother of God"* (Luther believed in the Immaculate Conception right up until his death.)

Was Mary without sin? I once asked a Franciscan priest why God would have granted Mary that grace and his response was, "If you had the power to protect your mother from the stain of original sin, wouldn't you?" I had to answer in the positive.

In the *Gospel of Luke* Gabriel refers to Mary as "full of grace" or "highly graced." The Greek word used is *kekaritomene*, a perfect passive particle meaning "you who are fully transfigured by grace," and it is not used of any other human being in Scripture. Here lies one indication of the Immaculate Conception.

Some Christians have argued that Mary's being sinless is impossible:

*Rom 3:23:* All have sinned and fall short of the glory of God.

*Ps 14:3:* They have all gone astray, they are all alike corrupt; there is none that does good, not even one.

The Greek word translated "all" (*pas*) doesn't universally mean "every single person without exception." For instance, Paul also says that "all Israel will be saved" (*Rom 11:26*), but clearly that does not mean "every single Jew without exception." We might note as well that Jesus, who was truly man, did not sin so Paul cannot mean "every human being has sinned." Also the words "all" and "many" are sometimes used interchangeably:

*Matt 20:28:* "The Son of Man came not to be served but to serve, and to give his life as a ransom for many."

*Mk 14:24:* "This is my blood of the covenant which is poured out for many."

Is Jesus saying that he didn't give his life for all of mankind or that his blood wasn't going to cover all our sins?

The lament of Psalm 14 is a matter of common Hebrew idiom; poetic, emotional and exaggerated language, not intended to be literal. This is clearly seen since the very next psalm talks about those who walk "without blame."

Other Christians object that if Mary was without sin then she didn't need Christ as her Savior. Mary seems to think otherwise since in her *Magnificat* she says, "My spirit rejoices in God my Savior." (*Lk 1:47*)

The Church teaches that Mary was saved *from* sin rather than *out of* sin; *preserved* rather than *delivered*. We are cleansed through the sacrament of Baptism. Mary was cleansed by a direct act of God in anticipation of Christ.

Here's an analogy: You're walking along a path and in the middle of it is a deep pit, you don't notice it and you fall in. A passerby pulls you out, saving you from the pit. Then a woman walks along this path and just as she's about to fall in, a passerby reaches out and pulls her back. She is also saved from the pit but before falling in, rather than after. Both people are saved from the pit, both have a savior.

*The New Eve*

*1 Cor 15: 45-49:* Thus it is written, "The first man Adam became a living being;" the last Adam became a life-giving spirit. But it is not the spiritual which is first but the physical, and then the spiritual. The first man was from the earth, a man of dust; the second man is from heaven. As was the man of dust, so are those who are of the dust; and as is the man of heaven, so are those who are of heaven. Just as we have borne the image of the man of dust, we shall also bear the image of the man of heaven.

Scripture refers to Christ as the new Adam and shows the parallels and contrasts. So who is the new Eve?

From the earliest times of the Church, Christians referred to Mary as the New Eve. (The Epistle of Mathatais the Diognetes, ca. 100AD, calls Mary "sinless" and the "New Eve;" Justin Martyr calls her the "New Eve" in his *Dialogue with Trypho*, 150AD.) Irenaeus, born about 130AD, who was taught by a disciple of John, wrote:

*As Eve was seduced by the speech of an angel, so as to flee God in transgressing his word, so also Mary received the good tidings by means of the angel's speech, so as to bear God within her, being obedient to this word. And, though the one had disobeyed God, yet the other was drawn to obey him; that of the virgin Eve, the virgin Mary might become the advocate and, as by a virgin the human race had been bound to death, by a virgin it is saved, the balance being preserved – a virgin's disobedience by a virgin's obedience.* (Against Heresies, 3, 19)

Though the term "New Eve" cannot be found in Scripture early witnesses testify to its use and there is a lot of support for it. Besides, the word "Trinity" is not in Scripture and wasn't even used until 181AD by Theophilus of Antioch, and yet we use the term in referring to God existing as Father, Son and Holy Spirit because there is much in Scripture that supports the doctrine.

*Gen 3:15:* I will put enmity between you and the woman, and between your seed and her seed; he shall bruise your head, and you shall bruise his heel.

This passage is referred to as the *protoevangelium* or "proto-Gospel" and the Church understood it to be the first promise of a coming Savior who would defeat the Enemy, and it says interesting things about the "woman."

The enmity between the woman and the serpent meant much more than just distaste or not liking one another. In Hebrew, enmity (*'e^bah*) meant hostile intention, total opposition; you shared no common ground. This is an enmity that *will* be placed between the woman and the serpent. It cannot mean Eve; she was not opposed to the serpent, they shared common ground. The woman referred to will be totally opposed to and will not listen to the serpent.

Note also that the passage refers to "her seed," a phrase found nowhere else in Scripture. This is very interesting since it was believed that seed and lineage came from the man, not from the woman.

The woman and her seed share the same enmity between the serpent and his seed, both are totally opposed to the serpent. The woman is Mary and her seed is Jesus Christ, who crushed the head of Satan.

Eve believed the serpent, disobeyed God, and sin and death entered the world. By the help of God she brought forth her firstborn son, Cain, who was a murderer.

Mary, the New Eve, believed the angel, obeyed God, and the conqueror of sin and death entered the world. By the power of the Holy Spirit she brought forth her firstborn Son, Jesus, who was the giver of life.

*Ark of the New Covenant*

The plan of the Ark of the Covenant is given to Moses in explicit detail in *Exodus 25:10-22*. It was to be made of the purest materials, was most sacred to the Israelites and it held a special place in their worship and warfare. God is described as being seated upon the cherubim above the cover and his Spirit overshadowing it in a special way. It was so sacred, in fact, that when David brought the ark to Jerusalem, Uzzah touched it and he died on the spot (*2 Sam 6:6, 7*).

According to legend Jeremiah hid the ark, altar and the sacred tent, and it would reappear before the coming of the Messiah.

*Jer 3:16:* When you multiply and become fruitful in the land, says the LORD, they will in those days no longer say, "The ark of the covenant of the LORD!" They will no longer think of it, or remember it, or miss it, or make another.

*2 Macc 2:5-7:* When Jeremiah arrived there, he found a room in a cave in which he put the tent, the ark, and the altar of incense; then he blocked up the entrance. Some of those who followed him came up intending to mark the path, but they could not find it. When Jeremiah heard of this, he reproved them: "The place is to remain unknown until God gathers his people together again and shows them mercy."

God showed his greatest act of love and mercy by sending his Son to die for humankind. The original ark was neither found nor remade because it contained the old covenant. Mary is the ark of the new covenant.

Upon bringing the ark to Jerusalem David was struck with fear and said, "How could the ark of the LORD come to me?" (*2 Sam 6:9*), and the ark remained in the house of Obededom the Gittite for three months. When Mary visits Elizabeth she is filled with joy and says, "And how does this happen to me, that the mother of my Lord should come to me?" (*Lk 1:43*), and just as David leapt for joy before the ark, John leapt in his mother's womb at the sound of Mary's voice and Mary remained with Elizabeth for three months.

The Ark of the Covenant was pure and sacred, for God overshadowed it and it carried the Word of God, Aaron's staff and the manna (*Heb 9:4*). Mary, the Ark of the New Covenant, was also kept pure and sacred, for the power of God overshadowed her and for nine months she carried in her womb the Word of God made flesh, our eternal high priest and the true Bread from Heaven.

**Perpetual Virginity**

*The deepening of faith in the virginal motherhood led the Church to confess Mary's real and perpetual virginity even in the act of giving birth to the Son of God made man. In fact, Christ's birth "did not diminish his mother's virginal integrity but sanctified it." And so the liturgy of the Church celebrates Mary as* Aeiparthenos, *the "Ever-virgin."* – CCC 499

*The Blessed Virgin Mary, who, as well after as when she brought him forth, continued a pure and unspotted virgin.* – John Wesley (founder of the Methodist Church), Letter to a Roman Catholic, 1749

Mary's remaining a virgin throughout her life was not seriously questioned until later in Protestantism. Even the early Protestant reformers Luther, Calvin and Zwingli taught that Mary was "ever-virgin," as confessed from the beginning by the Catholic Church. So why has this belief diminished among Protestants? Probably the same reason certain Christian sects have denied the virgin birth altogether: it requires much faith.

The only books of the New Testament that speak of the virginal conception of Christ are *Matthew* and *Luke*; the epistles of Paul and the *Gospel of Mark* are completely silent on the subject, and they're believed to be the earliest works of the New Testament. This silence causes people to think that the virgin birth stories came from later legends.

The virginal conception of Jesus was met with opposition and disbelief from Jews and pagans alike; it could not have derived from some pagan mythology to make Christianity more "likeable" or "believable." It's even more absurd to think that the Church just randomly made up the doctrine of the perpetual virginity when the Bible clearly speaks of Jesus's "brothers" and "sisters." A great faith is required to believe that Mary was a virgin when she birthed Christ. An even greater faith is required to believe that she remained a virgin.

*The "brothers" and "sisters" argument*

*Matt 15:55:* Is not this the carpenter's son? Is not his mother called Mary? And are not his brothers James and Joseph and Simon and Judas?

*Mk 6:3:* Is not this the carpenter, the son of Mary and brother of James and Joses and Judas and Simon, and are not his sisters here with us?

*Christ…was the only Son of Mary, and the Virgin Mother bore no more children besides Him…"brothers" really means "cousins" here, and Holy Writ and the Jews have always called cousins brothers.* – Martin Luther, Sermons on John, Ch. 1-4

In ancient Jewish and Near Eastern culture, the terms "brother" and "sister" were also applied to other relatives and not only to those who shared the same mother or father. This is seen in Abraham's referring to Lot as his brother (*Gen 13:8*) when in actuality Lot is his nephew, and Edomites being called brothers of

Israelites (*Deut 23:8*). Neither Hebrew nor Aramaic has a word that distinguishes "brother" from "cousin."

The Septuagint follows the Hebrew Scriptures and uses the word "brother" (*adelphos*) exclusively. The New Testament also uses the word exclusively, and the first Christians called each other "brothers," even when they were biologically unrelated.

When Jesus was twelve and went to Jerusalem with his parents, he is evidently the only son of Mary. It's very unusual to be an only child at that age, seeing as there wasn't any birth control. Notice also that in the above cited verses Christ is called "*the* son of Mary" rather than "one of Mary's sons;" nor is he called "one of the carpenter's sons," but "*the* carpenter's son."

The brothers that are named in *Matthew* and *Mark* are later identified as sons of another Mary (*Mt 27:56, Mk 15:40*), whom *John* calls "[Jesus's] mother's sister, Mary the wife of Clopas" (*Jn 19:25*). According to the early Christian historian Hegesippus, Clopas was the brother of Joseph, which would make these relatives cousins.

*John 7:3, 4:* His brothers said to him, "Leave here and go to Judea, so that your disciples also may see the works you are doing. No one works in secret if he wants to be known publicly. If you do these things, manifest yourself to the world."

Here the brothers advise like elders, which would be unthinkable for a younger sibling to do; it was a violation of respect and conduct. In first-century Jewish society, a younger brother would *never* tell his older brother what to do, especially the first-born brother.

Before Jesus dies he entrusts Mary to John, not a younger sibling (*Jn 19:26, 27*). If Mary had other sons she would have been put into the care of a family member, not an unrelated person. Some have argued that Jesus wanted Mary to be cared for by a disciple rather than a brother because his brothers did not believe in him (*Jn 7:5*). But surely Jesus knew that his brothers would become believers after the resurrection, seeing as they were present at the outpouring of the Spirit; not to mention St. James who became a leader of the Church in Jerusalem.

Those that insist the brothers of Christ are truly "blood brothers" are actually missing one important factor: The term "brother" *cannot* be taken literally because the closest relative Jesus could have would be a half-brother; Joseph was not his biological father.

*The first-born argument*

*Lk 2:7:* and [Mary] gave birth to her firstborn son.

The description of Jesus as "firstborn son" doesn't mean that Mary had other sons. Rather, it's a legal description indicating that Jesus possessed the rights and privileges of the firstborn. Later he is taken to Jerusalem and is presented to the Lord in accordance with the law that says, "Every male that opens the womb shall be consecrated to the Lord" (*Ex 13:2*).

*Ex 34:20:* All the first-born of your sons you shall redeem. And none shall appear before me empty.

The firstborn son was redeemed after he was born, not after a second child was born. "First-born" means just that: a son was born and he was the first. It doesn't imply a second. Just like I am my mother's firstborn son but I'm also her only son.

*The "until" argument*

*Matt 1:25:* [Joseph] had no relations with her until she bore a son, and he named him Jesus.

Many people argue that this verse clearly implies that Joseph had marital relations with Mary after Jesus was born but that is not the case. The purpose of this verse is not to inform us of Mary and Joseph's relations, but rather to emphasize that Joseph had nothing to do with the conception of Jesus.

The Greek word translated "until" (*heos*) does not indicate that the process changed or stopped after the event occurred. The word is also used to describe an on-going event. For example, the prophetess Anna was described as being a widow "until" she was eighty-four (*Lk 2:37*); that doesn't mean she got married later. There are similar uses of the word throughout Scripture.

*Matt 28:20:* "And behold, I am with you always, *until* the end of the age. (Emphasis added)

Of course, Jesus is not saying that he will no longer be with us after the end of the age. (Some translations read "even unto" rather than "until" though the word *heos* is being used.) Other passages refer to Jesus reigning until his enemies are placed under his feet (*Ps 110:1, 1 Cor 15:25*). If it *had* to mean an end to a previous state, then Christ would no longer be sitting at the right hand of the Father after his enemies are placed underfoot.

The use of the word "until" in these passages all indicate a continuous process. The Lord continues to be with us after the end of the age, he continues to sit at the Father's right hand after his enemies are placed under his feet, and Mary continued a pure, unspotted virgin after the birth of Christ.

**Assumption and Coronation**

*"Finally the Immaculate Virgin, preserved free from all stain of original sin, when the course of her earthly life was finished, was taken up body and soul into heavenly glory, and exalted by the Lord as Queen over all things, so that she might be more fully conformed to her Son, the Lord of lords and conqueror of sin and death." The Assumption of the Blessed Virgin is a singular participation of the resurrection of other Christians.* – CCC 966

Mary's bodily assumption into heaven is professed by both Catholic and Orthodox Churches. According to an ancient account of the life of St. Theodosius, the feast of the Assumption was already being celebrated in Palestine by the fifth century, indicating that this belief was well-established among the Christians who lived in the land where Jesus had spent his life.

Many Christians object to this belief because it's not in the Bible. However, the death of St. Joseph isn't described in Scripture either, though most people agree that he died before or during Jesus's public ministry. In fact, many events that surround Christ are not recorded in Scripture (*Jn 21:25*). And we mustn't forget that God took others to himself (Enoch and Elijah), and *Matthew* informs us of saints who rose from their tombs at the death of our Lord, so there's nothing "unbiblical" about the claim that God did the same thing for the woman who carried his Son, especially since she had the privilege of being preserved of original sin.

Another interesting point is that no city or church of the ancient world has ever claimed to be the burial place of Mary, nor has anyone claimed to have the bones of Mary, as many groups and churches have done with other saints. The early saints and fathers of the faith were held in high esteem. After their death, the bones of martyrs were collected and preserved by the early Christians. Mary was one of the first saints and yet no one ever claimed to have her remains. Best explanation for this is that it was known by all believers that Mary had been taken up bodily and was crowned the Queen of Heaven.

*Rev 12:1:* A great sign appeared in the sky; a woman clothed with the sun, with the moon under her feet, and on her head a crown of twelve stars.

The Church often connects this verse with Mary's coronation. In order to understand why Catholics revere Mary as the Queen of Heaven it's important to know about the position of queen mother.

The queen mother held a special position in the monarchy of Judah. For centuries before Christ, the queen of a Near Eastern kingdom was not the wife of a king, but a king's mother. This was partly due to the fact that a king would normally have multiple wives and concubines, but only one mother. She assisted the king in ruling over the land, was his counselor and even led the people in praise and worship. A shadow of Mary's role as queen mother and intercessor can be seen in Bathsheba.

Bathsheba was the mother of King Solomon. His brother, Adonijah, went to her and asked if she would intercede for him, requesting that Solomon would grant Abishag as his wife; Bathsheba agrees to speak on his behalf (*1 Kgs 2:12-18*).

*1 Kgs 2:19, 20:* Then Bathsheba went to King Solomon to speak to him for Adonijah, and the king stood up to meet her and paid her homage. Then he sat down upon his throne, and a throne was provided for the king's mother, who sat at his right. "There is one small favor I would ask of you," she said. "Do not refuse me." "Ask it, my mother," the king said to her, "for I will not refuse you."

Now Solomon was one of the most powerful and wisest kings in biblical history, but he is nothing compared to his descendent Jesus, the King of kings and Lord of lords. So if Solomon honored Bathsheba so highly as queen mother, how could we not expect that Jesus would do the same – if not more – in honoring Mary as his Mother? And just as Solomon was willing to grant his mother's requests, so Jesus responds to Mary's intercession.

One might object and say that in the end Solomon does not grant his mother's request but rather has Adonijah killed (*1 Kgs 2:25*). However, this is because that Abishag had been the concubine of David (*1 Kgs 1:4*), and Solomon inherited his father's harem. When Adonijah requested Abishag as his wife, he was subtly undermining the security of Solomon's throne; Solomon felt threatened by his brother so the request was not granted. This could be a reminder to Catholics that going to Mary with our requests is no guarantee that we will get what we want (as some people think). Only when our requests are not opposed to the will of her Divine Son will he not refuse her.

The title "Queen of Heaven" is hard for a lot of *sola scriptura* Christians to accept, which is understandable considering certain passages in *Jeremiah*:

*Jer 7:18:* The children gather wood, the fathers kindle fire, and the women knead dough, to make cakes for the queen of heaven; and they pour out drink offerings to other gods, to provoke me to anger.

*Jer 44:24-27:* Jeremiah said to all the people and all the women, "Hear the word of the LORD, all you of Judah who are in the land of Egypt: Thus says the LORD of hosts, the God of Israel: You and your wives have stated your intentions, and kept them in fact: 'We will continue to fulfill the vows we have made to burn incense to the queen of heaven and to pour out libations to her.' Very well! Keep your vows, carry out your resolutions! But listen then to the word of the LORD, all you people of Judah who live in Egypt; I swear by my own great name, says the LORD, in the whole land of Egypt no man of Judah shall henceforth pronounce my name, saying, 'As the Lord GOD lives.' I am watching over them to do evil, not good. All the men of Judah in Egypt shall perish by the sword or famine until they are utterly destroyed."

Jeremiah is rightly condemning the worship of the Assyro-Babylonian fertility goddess Ishtar, the daughter of the moon-god, who was called the queen of heaven. The baking of bread cakes in the shape of stars and the burning of incense were the way in which sacrifice was made to this goddess, who was associated with the planet Venus.

These pagans had a dim, fragmentary idea of God's ultimate truth. Just as the demi-gods of Greek and Roman legend, half-human, half-divine, are fragmentary images of the fully-human, fully-divine Christ, the fertility goddess is a very dim, fragmentary image of Mary, the Virgin who brought forth God incarnate.

In the first century there arose in Arabia the heresy of Collyridianism, which attempted to replace Ishtar with Mary. The followers declared Mary to be divine and offered her sacrifice, through the baking of bread cakes and the burning of incense as described in *Jeremiah*. The Church immediately condemned it as heresy and it has never revived.

In the Goth community there have been numerous people who were once involved in Wicca and paganism that have come into the Church. They have said that the honor and devotion that they give to Mary has been much more fulfilling than the worship that they gave a particular mother goddess or female deity; the

Mother of our Lord drew them closer to Christ rather than detracted them from him.

Never has the honor given to Mary by the Church been meant to be a form of worship or to diminish the mediation of Christ, but rather to emphasize it and show its power. Anytime that Mary has appeared to a saint or a group of people, such as Our Lady of Guadalupe, Fatima and Lourdes, she has professed her Son as her Lord and echoed the words she spoke at the wedding at Cana: "Do whatever he tells you." (*Jn 2:5*)

# Chapter 9:

# The Eucharist

*Ex 16:4, 31:* Then the LORD said to Moses, "I will now rain down bread from heaven for you"...The Israelites called this food manna.

Behold the Son of Manna, the true bread come down from Heaven: A poor, Jewish carpenter who not only claims to be God's Son, but also commands his disciples to gnaw on his flesh and drink his blood from a chalice. Though this sounds more like something Bela Lugosi would say as Dracula ("I never drink...wine."), the Eucharist instituted by Christ is considered the most blessed and holy sacrament of the Church.

The synoptic Gospels all record the institution of the Eucharist at the Last Supper, while *John* gives us the Bread of Life discourse that prepares for the Eucharist. St. Paul echoes the words of Jesus in the *First Letter to the Corinthians* (*1 Cor 11:23-26*). The Eucharist was central to early Christian worship.

All Christian churches celebrate the Eucharist or Communion in some way or another, but most denominations deny the Real Presence of Christ in the Eucharist. Some see the Eucharist only as a memorial, others see Christ as being spiritually present during the breaking of bread, and at best Christ is seen as being truly present in the bread and wine but his presence does not completely replace that of the host. Only the Eastern Orthodox and Catholic Churches adhere to the ancient belief that the bread and wine truly become the Body and Blood of Jesus Christ.

Understanding the Catholic doctrine of the Eucharist was a great barrier, alongside Mary, that I had to overcome before coming into full communion with the Church. I had celebrated Communion numerous times over the years in different churches and settings, and never once did I understand the words "This is my body" or "This is my blood" in a literal sense. I thought Jesus meant "This *represents* my body" or "This *means* my body" (as the Jehovah's Witnesses translate it.) But I learned that he did not mean either and that his words "This *is* my body" were truly what he meant.

The early Church Fathers testify that at the Last Supper when Jesus said the words they were understood in a literal sense:

St. Ignatius (110 AD): *"[heretics] abstain from Eucharist and from prayer because they do not confess that the Eucharist is the flesh of our Savior Jesus Christ." – Letter to Smyrnaeans 6, 2, 2*

St. Justin Martyr (150 AD): *"...not as common bread nor common drink do we receive these; but...as we have been taught, the food which has been made into the Eucharist by the Eucharistic prayer set down by him, and by the change of which our blood and flesh is nourished, is both the flesh and blood of that incarnated Jesus." – First Apology 66, 20*

St. Irenaeus of Lyons (195AD): *"[Jesus] has declared the cup, a part of his creation, to be his own blood, from which he causes our blood to flow; and the bread, a part of creation, he has established as his own body, from which he gives increase to our bodies." – Against Heresies 5, 2, 2*

But I reasoned, how could Jesus have been holding his own body and blood at the Last Supper? The Church Fathers all admitted that this was indeed a mystery, but it was accepted by faith that God has the power to perform such a miracle. This is one of the problems with Rationalism overtaking faith as "evidence of things not seen" (*Heb 11:2*). I then came to the realization that if the fullness of God can reside in the human Person of Jesus Christ, then surely he can transform bread and wine into the Body and Blood of our Savior while still retaining the appearances of bread and wine (called *transubstantiation*).

However, if Jesus truly is present under the forms of bread and wine, is he sacrificed again and again at every Mass? This couldn't be the case because Scripture clearly says that Christ was sacrificed "once for all" (*Heb 7:27*). I learned that the Eucharist is a *re-presentation* of Jesus' historical, one-time sacrifice for all. The priest re-enacts Jesus' priestly action at the Last Supper. He is not sacrificed *again* at Mass, but that sacrifice made "once for all" is made real and present here and now in the Eucharist, for it is a reality that transcends space and time, for Jesus' sacrifice is always present to God who does not exist in time as we do.

The objectors who continue to say that Jesus was only speaking symbolically tend to overlook many key passages and themes in the Scriptures:

*1 Cor 10:16*: The cup of blessing that we bless, is it not a participation in the blood of Christ? The bread that we break, is it not a participation in the body of Christ?

*1 Cor 11:27*: Therefore whoever drinks the cup of the Lord unworthily will have to answer for the body and blood of the Lord.

St. Paul doesn't just call the Eucharist a memorial of the death of Christ but rather a "participation" in his Body and Blood, and he later says that those who eat and drink without discerning the body of the Lord are eating and drinking judgment on themselves, and that a fair number of people had become ill and died for drinking unworthily (*1 Cor 11:29, 30*). That's quite a price to pay for the Eucharist to just be symbolic.

## The Lamb of God

When John the Baptist testifies to Jesus in the *Gospel of John* he refers to him as "the Lamb of God." (*Jn 1:29, 36*) The author of the gospel continues alluding to Jesus as the Passover lamb during his Passion narrative: Jesus is condemned to die on preparation day for Passover at noon (*Jn 19:14*), which according to John was the hour at which the priests began to slaughter the lambs for Passover. Then the climax at the crucifixion when Jesus was thrust through with a spear but his legs weren't broken, fulfilling the Scripture about the Passover lamb: "Not a bone of it will be broken." (*Ex 12:46*) St. Paul also calls Jesus the "paschal lamb who has been sacrificed," (*1 Cor 5:7*) and in *Revelation* Jesus appears as a "Lamb that seemed to have been slain" (*Rev 5:6*).

The early Church had no difficulty in seeing the Passover lamb as prefiguring the sacrifice of Christ on the cross. Just as the blood of the lamb protected the Israelites from death, the blood of Christ protects us from eternal damnation. And just as God commanded the Israelites to eat the Passover lamb, so did Jesus command his disciples to eat his flesh and drink his blood.

## The Bread of Life Discourse (Jn 6:22-71)

*Jn 6:30, 31*: So they said to him, "What sign can you do, that we may see and believe in you? What can you do? Our ancestors ate manna in the desert, as it is written: 'He gave them bread from heaven to eat.'"

The manna was thought to be hidden by Jeremiah along with the Ark of the Covenant (*2 Mac 2:5-8*) and it was expected to reappear miraculously at Passover in the last days. Jesus assures them that the manna has reappeared in the form of his flesh and blood.

*Jn 6:48-52*: "I am the bread of life. Your ancestors ate the manna in the desert, but they died; this is the bread that comes down from heaven so that one may eat it and not die. I am the living bread that came down from heaven; whoever eats this bread will live forever; and the bread that I will give is my flesh for the life of the world." The Jews quarreled among themselves, saying, "How can this man give us his flesh to eat?"

There are different times in the Gospels that Jesus speaks symbolically about food, but when it is misunderstood he clarifies himself. When he warns his disciples to beware of the leaven of the Pharisees and Sadducees, they take him literally and he rebukes them and they later understand that he meant to beware their teachings (*Mt 16:5-12*). When the Samaritan woman is told of the "living water" that Jesus offers she asks for this water so she doesn't have to continually go to the well (*Jn 4:15*), and it later becomes clear that the living water is the Spirit (*Jn 7:37-39*).

Notice that here Jesus does not rebuke the crowd for misunderstanding, but continues with what he originally said:

*Jn 6:53-56*: Jesus said to them, "Amen, amen, I say to you, unless you eat the flesh of the Son of Man and drink his blood, you do not have life within you. Whoever eats my flesh and drinks my blood has eternal life, and I will raise him on the last day. For my flesh is true food and my blood is true drink. Whoever eats my flesh and drinks my blood remains in me and I in him."

In verse 54 John starts using a different verb. While *phagos* means "to eat meat," the Greek word *trogos* means "to gnaw or munch." This could be John's way of emphasizing and re-emphasizing in the final verses the reality of the flesh and blood of Jesus. He is "true food and true drink," not symbolic food and drink.

There are places in the Old Testament that symbolically speak of eating flesh and drinking blood:

*2 Sam 23:17*: "Far be it from me, O LORD, that I should do this. Shall I drink the blood of the men who went at the risk of their lives?"

*Is 49:26*: I will make your oppressors eat their own flesh, and they shall be drunk with their own blood as with wine. Then all flesh shall know that I am the LORD your Savior, and your Redeemer, the Mighty One of Jacob.

To "eat the flesh and drink the blood" means to do someone serious injury. If Jesus were speaking metaphorically, he would be commanding his disciples to slander or assault him to gain eternal life. So the disciples understand him clearly, that he is commanding them to literally eat his flesh and drink his blood.

*Jn 6:60, 66*: Many of his disciples, when they heard it said, "This is a hard saying, who can listen to it?" After this many of his disciples drew back and no longer went about with him.

This is the only instance in Scripture in which disciples leave Jesus. They were not an unbelieving crowd, they were true disciples that had followed Jesus and witnessed miracles. But this was just too much for them. If Jesus were only speaking symbolically would he have truly let them return to their old lives? Would he not have rebuked them and clarified himself saying, "Wait! I was only speaking in a parable!" He did not do so because they understood him correctly and could not accept the possibility of eating the flesh and blood of Christ.

I accepted the possibility of Jesus truly being present in the Eucharist. When I first partook of the Blessed Sacrament I was reminded of when I accepted Christ as my Lord and Savior; the euphoria that came over me. In receiving the Eucharist I was filled with awe as I felt Christ in a new form. Not only present in spirit, but now his Body and Blood ran through my body and blood. "One bread, one body."

## Chapter 10:

## My Journey as a Gothlic

Meeting the local bishop for the first time is quite memorable. He just happened to be at my church one night, talking to different people and I noticed he kept looking over at me. (This is when I still had all my facial piercings, wore eyeliner all the time and was adorned with spikes and chains; proclaiming my "Gothicity" to its fullest.) He started walking in my direction and I thought, Oh God, he's gonna ask me what I'm doing in this church. But what happens? He picks up the big silver cross necklace off my chest and says, "Man! You wanna trade? It's bigger than mine!"

After just a few months of entering the Catholic Church I was shocked when I realized I received less opposition from Catholics about being Gothic than I had from any other Christians. I was even asked to go on Realife Radio, the local Catholic radio station, to talk about coming into full communion and the Gothic subculture. About a week later I went to a Mass and a woman came up and asked if I was the one on the radio. She informed me that she really enjoyed the discussion and that it opened her mind. I would be told similar things by many more Catholics over the years.

The relationship I was in upon entering the Church crumbled after a year. Not even two months later I met a girl online and thought I'd found the girl I was supposed to marry. I packed all my belongings into a Uhaul and moved down to Georgia to begin a new relationship. After being homeless and unemployed for three months and learning that the girl was mentally-unstable I realized I made a mistake, and was forced to move back to Kentucky and to live with my mother and sisters until I got reestablished.

As soon as I returned to Kentucky I felt like I needed to spend some alone time with God so I scheduled a retreat at the Trappist monastery, the Abbey of Gethsemani; a week of silence, prayer and meditation. My first thought when I got there was, am I really going to be able to go a week without a phone, TV or CDs? It only took five minutes of being on those grounds to not even think about those devices again.

The time that I spent with the monks, chanting psalms, praying the Rosary, receiving the Eucharist daily and reading the Word enabled me to listen to the Holy Spirit. The Lord revealed to me that I was addicted to relationships; I was always either in one or single and looking, never content with being single. In five years I went through four different relationships and none of them were chaste, and my relationship with each woman was damaging my relationship with Christ. I made a promise to God at that monastery. I vowed to remain single for at least a year, and to restore my relationship with him before entering one with a woman. After that year was over I was so content with being single I didn't even bother to try dating again.

Living with my mom and sisters again was not a very pleasant experience, but I had no money and no other options. It wasn't too long after returning, however, that I got a job at the Toyota manufacturing plant, and because I had no car my cousin picked me up for work every day. The money started coming in and I began saving to get a car and an apartment. It was also at this time that I had to do one of the most difficult things of my life: press charges against my own mother.

While I was in college my mother had put five credit cards in my name, maxing them all out and destroying my credit. My credit was so horrible that I couldn't even get approved for a cell phone. When I confronted her about it and explained that I had to take action she played the victim, made me out to be the bad guy and even threatened suicide if I did such a thing.

Other family members were supportive, informing me that my mom had stolen from almost every family member over the years and that she also had a drug problem. Upon learning these things I knew she had to suffer the consequences of her actions if she was to receive any help. Mom ended up in jail for a few months, my sisters moved in with my grandmother and I moved out on my own.

Finally living on my own with no roommate, no financial difficulties and a steady job seemed like a dream come true; things were coming together at last. My passion for music gave birth to my album, *Eden's Graveyard*, under my Goth name Reverend Leviathan. It was received well in the Goth community and I was surprised when some of my musical icons also complimented it.

My passion to be more involved in the Church really began to grow. I learned about the Knights of Columbus and was very intrigued by their emphasis on unity, charity, fraternity and patriotism; I became a first degree knight in November 2008. Two years later I would be honored with the highest degree.

As a knight my spiritual life seemed to be flourishing, but my economical life was not doing as well. After working at Toyota for a year I was laid off due to a recall in cars, thus putting me on unemployment. They brought me back a few months later, another year passed and I was laid off once again, this time due to my epilepsy causing me to miss so many days at work. So I was forced to move in with my cousin and his family and I worked many odd jobs afterwards, trying to discover my vocation and calling in life.

During my struggles with employment I tried to read more books on spirituality and mysticism. I soon discovered a work by St. John of the Cross entitled *Dark Night of the Soul* (a title very appealing to almost any Goth). The book had a strong impact on me and after reading it I began thinking about religious life, and much to my surprise I had a peace about the possibility of entering a religious community. My closest friends, most of whom aren't Catholic, were all encouraging me; including a former teacher who is a devout atheist. When you have an atheist encouraging you to join a religious order, wouldn't you say that means something? After reading a Benedictine monk's testimony on the back of *Columbia* magazine I knew I had to follow this desire. My first stop was where the article was from: St. Vincent Archabbey in Latrobe, Pennsylvania.

I found St. Vincent Archabbey to be very beautiful and the monks and vocation director to be very Spirit-filled, loving people. Two days there had me praying that God intended for me to enter that order. However, at the end of the weekend the vocation director informed that I couldn't be considered because I didn't have a college degree; all the monks there are expected to teach at the school connected to the monastery. I was very disappointed and my hopes were flying out the window. As I was writing in my journal I thought to myself, "What am I to do, Lord," and for whatever reason I scribbled out the letter to each word on the side of my journal which came out as "WAITDL." I saw the word "wait" and felt encouragement to not give up my search just because one community rejected me.

My next "come and see" weekend was spent at St. Meinrad in Indiana. The vocation director was very concerned about my tattoos and piercings, and as I told him about myself he said I sounded more like a Franciscan than Benedictine. Now since I'd only been Catholic for a few years I didn't really know what the differences were in religious orders so I did some research and saw a lot of myself in St. Francis of Assisi, and I felt more called to an active rather than contemplative life, so I contacted the vocation director at St. Anthony friary in Cincinnati. To save myself from another hurt of rejection I came straight out and told the Franciscan priest about my involvement in the Goth community, my tattoos and piercings and he said it wasn't an issue.

It's true what they say sometimes that the third time's a charm. I felt more peace and confirmation about St. Anthony than I did at the previous communities, and the more I learned about the Franciscan order the more I wanted to be a part of it. I felt a strong spiritual connection with St. Francis of Assisi. At the end of the weekend when I was called in to meet with the vocation director I hoped for the best and prepared for the worst. I told him how I felt about my experience and he said, "Well, Shane, I'll be perfectly honest with you...I definitely see you having a future with us." He handed me the folder containing all of the information I needed to fill out and I returned home praising God that weekend.

Preparing for the postulancy seemed more like I was entering the FBI or military; providing them with information about my birth, parents, baptism, physical and dental exam, etc. It was also at this time that I became part of The Grave Robbers, a Christian Gothic ministry dedicated to sharing the Gospel with those in the Gothic subculture; something I could do alongside being at the friary.

Though my family didn't quite understand the decision I was making they were all supportive over the next few months as I filled out all the paperwork and waited to go before the review board in the spring of 2011.

The "Franciscan committee" had a couple concerns before welcoming me. First they asked me if I'd be willing to remove my facial piercings. If they said it was because they were sinful I would've left, but they said it was because in the community we need to be mindful of the weak-minded and that many people wouldn't understand; I agreed that I could part with them. Also they wanted to know about a previous addiction to pornography that I had struggled with, and I told them it had been conquered. So after their review they decided I was a good candidate and I would begin my discernment as a postulant in August. There were eight men that were accepted into postulancy, though only six of us entered.

My first couple days at St. Anthony friary were a blessing. After arriving and seeing the size of my room I realized I'd brought way too much stuff if I was going to become a friar so I got rid of a lot of my decorative items (gargoyles, posters, novelties) and DVDs. Interesting thing was it didn't bother me. I had a peace about parting with it and was reminded of the words of my Lord, "Sell *all* you have and follow me."

The postulant director, Father Carl, and all of the other friars seemed extremely nice. When I met my fellow postulants – Matt, Will, Josh, Clay and Jeff – I saw that we were a very diverse group of men but we were all bonded by the same calling: to discern the possibility of following the way of St. Francis of Assisi.

The welcoming ceremony was beautiful. The provincial director, Father Jeff, proceeded over it and some other friars from out of town were present. We were each presented a Tau cross, and then one by one the friars presented us with a sign of peace. That sense of love and acceptance just confirmed even more that God wanted me to be a part of that community.

Over the next couple of months we would begin our classes on Franciscan spirituality, theology and Church history. At times it felt like being back in college again. We were each given a chore to do in the friary; mine was cleaning the community bathroom on one end of the hall. We also chose someone as a spiritual director. I would meet with a Poor Clare by the name of Sister Anna Marie once a month. We had our times of fellowship, prayer, class and Mass. In such a short period we all felt so close to one another, and then came the big tragedy.

In the month of October our fellow postulant Matt was sent to the hospital in a lot of pain. As it turns out he had suffered from melanoma in the past, it had spread and it was severe. We were informed that with chemotherapy he would have six months to a year of life, without it two to six months; Matt refused chemo and decided to return to New York to spend his remaining time with his family. Two months later we received word that he died and we attended his funeral. Though we'd only been together for a brief time we spent most of that time together, and we all felt that we truly lost a close brother.

Shortly after Matt's death it was time to pick a ministry that we would attend to once a week. We were given a variety of things to choose from; Will and I both chose to volunteer at the Little Sisters of the Poor nursing home. Every Thursday I would spend time with the residents, helping them to therapy and Mass, and playing games with them. It was very fulfilling being able to bring joy to these elderly people (and sometimes a bit frightening with the occasional old lady that would hit on me and call me sexy).

The mid-year evaluation in January was a turning point for me in formation. The community said each of us would be called in individually to receive feedback from the friars about how well we're doing as postulants. We were told that it would all be done in the spirit of charity which took some pressure off of me, but when I was called in it felt more like the spirit of judgment.

Though no one addressed this as a problem for the first few months I was there, everyone had something to say about my being Gothic. One friar admitted that he probably just didn't understand but then said he didn't see Christ in the way I presented myself. Another one went so far as saying, "I can't believe you were accepted into the program" and "drop the Goth shit." Other men said they saw growth and potential, and also that I seemed very intelligent. I was supposed to be able to respond afterwards but right after the final friar spoke they called a five minute break.

I felt horrible after my evaluation. I knew I was going to receive some criticism but I expected it to be more constructive, and I also thought I'd get more compliments. The other postulants were shocked when I told them what was said. That night I very strongly considered leaving the friary. I couldn't understand why I was expected to change who I was rather than them change their perspective of me. Later that night both Will and Father Bonaventure came to my door with words of encouragement. Will was very saddened to hear I was considering leaving, and Bonaventure reassured me of the positive aspects he saw in me and urged me to press on.

I spoke with many different people about the evaluation. Most seemed to agree that I wasn't being asked to change who I was but rather to tone down certain aspects. I was still a little uncomfortable with that idea but others were telling me it was of little importance, including those in the Goth community. Brian Healy, lead singer of Dead Artist Syndrome and godfather of Christian Goth music said, "Dude, so what if you're being asked to tone down your appearance? Go buy a couple colored t shirts and wear one once a week!" Skot Shaw, lead singer of Leper said, "You are not 'Shane the Goth,' you are 'Shane the Servant of God.' You are always going to be you no matter what changes you make." Here were fellow Goths telling me that I didn't need to see this as selling out or conforming to the close-minded; I was sacrificing a small aspect of the subculture for a greater good.

A week after the evaluation I met with Father Frank. He took off his habit and said, "Shane, am I any less a Franciscan when I'm not wearing this?" I responded in the negative and he said, "So why would you be any less of a Goth if you just toned down your appearance?" Then I realized that it had finally happened: Gothic aesthetics had become a vanity for me. It had almost gotten to the point that my identity as a Goth was primary and my identity as a

Catholic was secondary. The Lord's words – "Why are you so anxious about clothes?" – took on a whole new meaning. I also reflected on the story of the rich man and I knew I didn't want to be like him; walking away sad, unwilling to sacrifice his goods and follow Jesus. I made the decision to not be so "in your face" about being Gothic and to continue on my journey as a postulant.

The next few months that would follow brought about many changes in me and the community. Our fellow postulant, Clay, discerned that the Franciscan life was not for him and he left formation. I began counseling and working on my areas that needed growth and preparing myself for a more "normal" attire. I noticed that as I met new people and they asked me about my interests, when I would bring up the Goth scene they seemed more open to listen, since they did not judge me right off the bat.

When I attended The Grave Robbers' Black Carpet event I saw my friend Jeremy whom I hadn't spoken with since Thanksgiving. He informed me that I seemed much more at peace with myself than our previous meeting; that the last time we saw each other I appeared to have a dark cloud over my head. Jeremy realized when he last saw me that I was attempting to live two lives, to form a marriage between the Gothic and Franciscan lifestyles. Now he saw that I was devoting myself more to the life I was choosing.

Though a couple friars admitted that they witnessed growth in me, they questioned its authenticity; they wondered if I was just "jumping through hoops." I defended myself saying that I wasn't one to do that and that I wanted to continually grow, not just meet their standards and then stop. Although I had grown I feared that it wasn't going to be good enough to continue in formation and that I'd be asked to leave. After worrying about that possibility for a few days I came to a point that I would accept whatever happens with a sense of peace; either thanking God for a year of growth and reflection or thanking him for allowing me to continue my discernment.

Exactly one day after I received peace about whatever decision would be made I was called into a meeting with Fathers Frank and Carl. They informed me that it was determined that I wouldn't continue onto Novitiate. However, they offered me the opportunity to continue Postulancy for another year, living at a different friary in Cincinnati. They reassured me that they'd seen great progress and that they saw a lot of potential, but that I probably wasn't ready for Novitiate.

I was surprisingly pretty calm as I spoke with them, and I didn't see their decision as a punishment but a privilege; they rarely offered that option. As soon as I placed my formation in God's hands he gave it right back to me and said, "You must make the decision." Since the door was not closed just yet I chose to accept their offer and finish out my year at St. Anthony.

Before entering the next Franciscan community I did have a final evaluation and I was very pleased; it was a complete one eighty. Each of the friars said they'd seen tremendous growth and progress, informed me how much of an impact I had made on their community and they were glad that I accepted the offer to continue my discernment. I finished my last few months at St. Anthony and then moved into St. Clare that summer.

St. Clare friary was much different than St. Anthony. I was allowed to get a part-time job since I wasn't going to be taking any classes, and I also continued my ministry. But as time went on I started to think about leaving. One of the greatest aspects I loved about the Franciscan life was the sense of community, which seemed to disappear. There were only four of us at the friary, we rarely saw each other and only recited Evening Prayer together. The sense of community began to vanish along with my sense of peace.

During this time I was also talking a lot more with my close friend Amelia. In this time of confusion we started to grow closer in our friendship and we both admitted to having strong feelings for one another. Due to my experiences in previous relationships I did not want a woman to be one of the reasons for my leaving, but I also couldn't deny the emotions I was experiencing. We agreed that we would spend two weeks in prayer about these issues, and that I would talk to my friends and superiors about my desires.

I found myself very conflicted. I couldn't leave for the wrong reasons, but I also couldn't stay for the wrong reasons. My reasons for staying were not very good: I had a sense of security at the friary and feared having to start fresh in the world; I didn't want to hear "I knew you wouldn't stay" and other criticisms from certain family members, and I was afraid of beginning a new relationship. Fear was the greatest factor keeping me in formation. The only peace that seemed to remain was my connection with St. Francis and Franciscan spirituality. My spiritual director, Sister Anna Marie, mentioned the possibility of becoming a secular Franciscan and being in a relationship; that I could apply Franciscan spirituality to my daily life without entering an order. Other people I spoke with said they admired me for even trying out the Franciscan lifestyle and that I shouldn't see myself as a failure. I concluded (very hesitantly) that entering the Franciscan order was not my vocation. I left formation and began my relationship with Amelia.

People have asked me numerous times if I regret ever entering Postulancy and the answer is absolutely not. There is not a doubt in my mind that God intended for me to discern the possibility of religious life. I heard the calling to enter the process and was obedient to that voice, but obedience is only the beginning; what God wants from our obedience may be completely contrary to what we want from it. I wanted to become a friar, but he used it to shape me into a better man. I tell people that during my year there I was the rich demoniac named Abraham. First, I was the rich man who wanted to follow Jesus but was about to walk away sad when I was asked to give up the things that I loved (Gothic aesthetics, relationships, material possessions). Then I was Abraham, willing to sacrifice that which was dearest to me, and right as I was raising the knife God stopped me when I reached the point of realizing that he was the most important aspect of my life. Lastly, just like the demoniac, after I was healed of a "Legion" of demons I begged to stay with Jesus in the friary but he said, "Go home to your family and announce to them all that the Lord in his pity has done for you." (*Mk 5:19*)

Upon leaving formation I moved to Eighty Four, Pennsylvania, where Amelia and I would begin our relationship. Once again the problems of employment were haunting me, as I had maybe four jobs in three months. I kept trying to get established with very little success, and realized that I had to return to Kentucky because I had neither family nor stability in Pennsylvania. Amelia and I had grown to love each other so we decided that we would continue our relationship long distance for awhile, seeing each other once a month.

When I returned to Kentucky my aunt and uncle allowed me to stay with them in Georgetown until I got reestablished, which didn't take too long. I soon had my own place and a job at Aichi Forge. However, the job didn't last long because I had a petite seizure on the assembly line and I was forced to leave, put on restraint from driving and no working around heavy machinery. I put in a few applications at different places and ended up as a part-time employee at Wal-Mart, seeing as it was in walking distance from my apartment.

It is true that the grass is always greener on the other side of the fence. Being hit with familiar problems caused me to doubt my decision to leave formation and the desire to enter a religious order once again began weighing heavy on my mind. I informed Amelia of this and though I assured her of my love I felt that it was best to put our relationship on hold until I figured out what my true calling in life was. Three weeks later came the next life-altering (and threatening) experience that provided me with the answer.

I could no longer afford health insurance with the pay decrease at Wal-Mart and I wouldn't be eligible for benefits until I was a full-time employee. So I was left with a month's supply of medication and when I ran out I just prayed that God would protect me from seizures. I went three days without any medication and was hit with a rude awakening quite literally:

I was awakened on a Saturday morning by a bunch of knocking at my door. My first thought was that it was the maintenance man. As I attempted to get out of bed I noticed my body was very weak and sore, my tongue was swollen and I had lost bladder control; all indications of seizure activity. I got dressed and slowly walked into the living room to discover my coffee table knocked over and the cushions on my loveseat were all messed up. I didn't want whoever was at the door to think that there was a drunken brawl in my apartment so I attempted to reset the coffee table but was far too weak. I only had enough strength to straighten up the loveseat, which I discovered was wet, indicating multiple seizures.

I finally made it to the door while the frantic knocking continued, and I opened it to my managers from Wal-Mart and a police officer. I was suffering a bit of amnesia at the time and though I recognized them I didn't know who they were. Laurie looked at me and said, "Oh thank God! Here, it's Amelia," and handed me her cell phone.

Amelia was hysterical on the phone, crying and asking if I was okay. I did my best to explain that I'd had a seizure but I sounded like someone who'd just had a stroke, very slurred and slow. She asked me what was the last thing I remembered us talking about and I went over our last phone conversation to which she responded, "That was two days ago." I was very confused, picked up by an ambulance and taken to the hospital.

The doctors would discover that the seizures began on Thursday night, two or three occurring, and I was completely out of it till I was picked up that morning. Amelia had grown concerned when she tried contacting me numerous times on Friday with no success, and my managers were worried when I didn't show up for work on Saturday and they couldn't get a hold of me either. So when Amelia called Wal-Mart looking for me everyone knew something was wrong. She then called 911, was redirected to Kentucky since she was out of state, and my managers rushed to my apartment to wait for EMS.

I was in the emergency room for about an hour or two then I was picked up by my mom and her boyfriend. Seeing that I still wasn't well enough to be left alone they took me to my aunt and uncle's house. Even after a few hours my symptoms hadn't changed so my aunt Becky suggested I stay with them until I was fully recuperated. Little did we know that it would take four days.

Later that night my uncle Rodney was asking me why I didn't have any medication and I slowly explained that I couldn't afford it. In a very concerned and somewhat disappointed tone he began saying I should have informed someone and gotten some assistance, that someone – even he – would have helped me to get my medicine. I could sense that he was just as scared as I was about my condition so I got up and wrapped my arms around him; we both cried in each other's arms. Probably only the second time in my life I've seen that man cry.

Though I was able to think clearly I was not able to communicate my thoughts very well, especially with my wounded tongue. Because it was taking me longer than usual to recuperate I was very worried about suffering permanent brain damage; being stuck with having to nod "yes" or "no" to questions and comments, having to make hand gestures to express myself and having unbalanced emotions. But those fears would soon fade with the miracles that followed.

On the third night of my stay at my uncle's house I noticed my body felt very heavy and weighed down, like I was carrying something, but simultaneously I felt weightless and free. I then heard a voice say, "That's the weight of the cross."

Sitting in the kitchen I was reflecting on what I heard and I looked down at the front door, and in the door I could clearly see the reflection of someone kneeling down on the steps praying. I looked away, rubbed my eyes and looked back, and he was still there. I walked up to the steps to find no one, but again I looked at the glass door and reflected on the steps was this person praying. Whether it was an angel or a saint I don't know but he appeared to be wearing a dazzling Franciscan habit.

I went into the living room and sat down on the couch praying, "Okay, Lord, this isn't happening for no reason. What are you trying to show me here?" My cousin was watching TV and changed the channel; a comedian was talking about drinking, staying away from liquor and just sticking to beer (something I'd been attempting for awhile since I only ever drank too much when it came to hard liquor). He changed the channel again and there was a commercial about how dangerous it is to go without your medication and to apply for assistance. Then a program came on and a guy was talking about a woman he loved and trying to figure out whether or not he should be with her.

    I laughed and cried at the irony of God using the TV to speak to me while my cousin just looked at me like I was nuts, and then came that same peaceful voice I heard before. He said, "Your desire to enter religious life is indeed pure, there are no false motivations. But you must let go of this desire; you can do far greater things for me and my kingdom out here. You must take the greater challenge."

    A feeling of peace was overflowing in my entire body after hearing that, along with some disappointment and fear; disappointed that I wasn't called to enter an order, and afraid of what this "greater challenge" might be. As I lay in bed unable to sleep, pondering all of what happened to me and being unsure of everything, the word "faith" flashed in front of my eyes, lighting up the room and then fading away. Not shortly after there were luminous beings walking around the bed, almost like they were keeping watch over me. Again, when I tried to look directly at one I couldn't see anyone, but the others remained in my peripheral vision.

    Never in my life did I ever think having multiple seizures would be considered a blessing. Normally after a seizure I'd find myself thinking, "Really, Lord? Why do you refuse to heal me?"

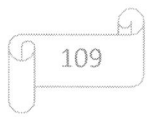

But this time all I could do was praise him for this experience and thank him for using this thorn in my side to communicate his will to me.

Two weeks after returning home I told Amelia that there was no point in denying or delaying it; we loved each other and should be together since it was revealed to me that I wasn't meant for Holy Orders. (We would later be joined in marriage.) The same day that we were reunited I was informed that if my managers hadn't come to my apartment that Saturday morning I would've been dead a day or two later due to my level of dehydration.

I reflected on the possibility of being dead and I started wondering, why are people constantly coming to my rescue? Why am I blessed with so many people that care about me? Why was I spared death when there are far better people than me in the world? I was then struck with an extreme sense of God's love and my own unworthiness, and I broke down and cried; finally willing to accept his plan and not my own.

In the words of Thomas Merton, I have no idea where I am going, and just because I think that I am following God's will it doesn't mean that I am actually doing so, but I believe that the desire to please the Lord does in fact please him, and I hope to do nothing apart from that desire. For me that desire lies in ministry; in the Church and the Goth community. I continue this journey as a "Gothlic" with my renewed faith and revelation: My faith comes before my fashion, my Master before my music, my God before my Goth. I'm not a devout Goth that just so happens to be Catholic; I'm a devout Catholic that just so happens to be Goth.

# Acknowledgments

I had a lot of support and assistance in the production of this book, and I'd like to start by thanking my beautiful wife, Amelia, for her patience with me and also for designing the front cover. You are the next chapter in my life, beginning when this book ended, so you'll be in the second edition or my next book. Love you.

A big thank you to Mike and "Goth Mom" Donna Sheehy of the Grave Robbers. You all gave me much encouragement and made it possible for this book to finally be in print. May God strengthen the ministry and take us to higher places.

Discerning religious orders was a very important chapter in my life and I am eternally grateful for Father Carl Langenderfer and the friars of St. Anthony friary in Cincinnati. Thank you for accepting me and enduring me for my year of postulancy. Once I get famous you can put a plaque by the door of my old room.

My former theology professors, Dr. Kevin Anderson and Dr. Owen Dickens, were a big help when it came to clarifying/correcting my Greek and Hebrew. Even ten years later you're still educating me.

Cheers to Aurelio Voltaire! You are awesome for letting me quote from *What is Goth?* and for using a previous statement you said about me. Oh my, Goth! Hope to see you again soon.

Meagan Ewton, you were the first person to review my rough draft and tell me how bad it was. So hopefully this final edition is better than what you first read.

I think I speak for a lot of people in the Christian Goth community when I say we are blessed to have someone like Michaela Johnson, the web mistress of ChristianGoth.com. Thank you for posting many sources and testimonies, especially ones that helped with my section of "Problems Only Christian Goths Have."

Jeremy Hanke, my friend and "boss" of Darkest Goth magazine. You're acknowledged so I can get some ad space. God bless you and your family, my friend.

The cover of the book would be blank if it weren't for my old friend, Zac Hiler, who brought my wife's design to life. You're an awesome photographer and computer designer. Let's keep up the team work for future video blogs.

Definitely have to thank my supervisor, Brandon Craft, for allowing me to work on my book when we didn't have trucks to stock.

Last, but of course not least, I want to thank my friends and family who have patiently waited to read this for over a year. Any of you who once asked me, "So when's your book coming out," you were driving me to finish it. If I've forgotten someone or you want to be thanked personally for a particular reason, here you go: Thank you_____ for _____.

Christ's peace be upon you,<br>
Reverend Leviathan<br>
Psalm 30

Made in the USA
Middletown, DE
13 May 2021